Design Principles of Operating System: A Complete Reference

Dr.K. Kumaravel, MCA., M.Phil, CCNA., Ph.D.,

Professor & Head

Department of Computer Science

Dr.N.G.P. Arts and Science College (Autonomous),

Coimbatore, Tamil Nadu.

Published by

Design Principles of Operating System: A Complete Reference

ISBN 978-93-86638-47-2

Author

Dr.K. Kumaravel

Bonfring

309, 2nd Floor, 5th Street Extension, Gandhipuram,

Coimbatore-641 012.

Tamilnadu, India.

E-mail: info@bonfring.org

Website: www.bonfring.org

Phone: 0422 4213231

Preface

Operating systems are an essential part of any computer system. Similarly, a course on operating systems is an essential part of any computer science education. This field is undergoing rapid change, as computers are now prevalent in virtually every arena of day-to-day life— from embedded devices in automobiles through the most sophisticated planning tools for governments and multinational firms. Yet the fundamental concepts remain fairly clear, and it is on these that we base this book. We wrote this book as a text for an introductory course in operating systems at the junior or senior undergraduate level or at the first-year graduate level. We hope that practitioners will also find it useful. It provides a clear description of the concepts that underlie operating systems.

Understanding the main principles and algorithms underlying a modern operating system is essential in undergraduate computer science. The complexity of this subject, however, means that mastering it requires significant practical experience. This unique book accomplishes just that: it teaches introductory subjects in OS design and implementation through hands-on engagement with OSP 2, the next generation of the highly popular OSP courseware. The fundamental concepts and algorithms covered in the book are often based on those used in both commercial and open-source operating systems. Our aim is to present these concepts and algorithms in a general setting that is not tied to one particular operating system. However, we present a large number of examples that pertain to the most popular and the most innovative operating systems, including Linux, Microsoft Windows, Apple Mac OS X, and Solaris. We also include examples of both Android and iOS, currently the two dominant mobile operating systems.

This book exposes students to many essential features of operating systems while at the same time isolating them from low-level, machine-dependent concerns. With its accompanying software, the book contains enough projects for up to three semesters. Even one semester's study, however, suffices to cover page-replacement strategies in virtual memory management, CPU scheduling strategies, disk seek-time optimization and other issues in operating system design.

Dr.K. Kumaravel

Acknowledgement

I would like acknowledge the authors of various textbooks on Digital Communication & Communication networking whose presentation ideas benefited me both directly and indirectly while writing this book. I am thankful to the reviewers of this book for their valuable comments; suggestions put forth me to develop the book in a good way and their feedback improves me with new ideas & concepts. I whole heartedly thank the publishers for their support and cooperation. I am thankful to my faculty and my students who kindled in me the idea of writing for them. I thank my wife and my son for their constant support, enthusiasm, encouragement and understanding. I am thankful to all my family members for their continuous support.

Dr.K. Kumaravel

About the Author

Dr.K.Kumaravel serving as a professor & Head, Dr.N.G.P. Arts & Science. He have more than two decades in teaching and Research Experience. He contributed more than 40 Research Publications in various International Journals and presented 17 papers in various International/National conferences, seminars, and symposium. He has good potential in Academic and Research area. He gave invited talks in various abroad conferences, seminars. and guest talks to various institutions and also member in Board of Studies in Computer Science. He is a reviewer and Member in Editorial Board in International Journal for Computer Communication & Networks and also member in International Association for Academic Researchers (INAAR).

<table>
<tr><td>Chapter</td><td>Contents</td><td>Page No</td></tr>
</table>

CHAPTER 1

INTRODUCTION

A modern computer consists of one or more processors, some main memory, disks, printers, a keyboard, a mouse, a display, network interfaces, and various other input/output devices. All in all, a complex system. If every application programmer had to understand how all these things work in detail, no code would ever get written. Furthermore, managing all these components and using them optimally is an exceedingly challenging job. For this reason, computers are equipped with a layer of software called the operating system, whose job is to provide user programs with a better, simpler, cleaner, model of the computer and to handle managing all the resources just mentioned. These systems are the subject of this book.

1.1.   Definition of Operating System

An Operating system is a program that controls the execution of application programs and acts as an interface between the user of a computer and the computer hardware.

A more common definition is that the operating system is the one program running at all times on the computer (usually called the kernel), with all else being applications programs.

An Operating system is concerned with the allocation of resources and services, such as memory, processors, devices and information. The Operating System correspondingly includes programs to manage these resources, such as a traffic controller, a scheduler, memory management module, I/O programs, and a file system.

1.2.   History of Operating Systems

First Generation (1945–1955)

1) Vacuum Tubes
2) Plug boards

In this generation, all succeeded in building calculating engines. In earlier days mechanical relays were used they were very slow, with cycle time which as measured in seconds. Relays were later replaced by vacuum tubes. These machines were enormous, filling up entire rooms with tens of thousands of vacuum tubes, but they were still millions of times slower than even the cheapest personal computers available today. In those earliest days a single group of people designed, built, programmed, operated and maintained each machine. All programming was done in absolute machine language, by often writing up plug boards to control the machine's basic functions. Programming languages were unknown (even assembly language was unknown).

The Second Generation (1955–1965)

1) Transistors
2) Batch system

The introduction of the transistors in the mid of 1950s changed the picture radically. Computers became reliable enough that they could be manufactured and sold to paying customers with the expectation that they could continue to function long enough to get some useful work done for the first time, there was a clear separation between designers, builders, operators, programmers and maintenance personnel. These machines are now called main frame computers.

When the computer finished whatever job it was currently running, an operator would go over to the printer and teen off the output and carry it over to the output room, so that the programmer could collect it later. Then he would take one of the card decks that had been brought from the input room and read it in. If the FORTAN computer was needed, the operator have to get it from the file cabinet and read it in. Much computer time was wasted while operators were walking around the machine room. Given the high cost for the equipment, it is not surprising that people quickly looked for ways to reduce the wasted time. The solution generally adopted was the batch system.

The Third Generation (1965-1980)

1) ICs
2) Multiprogramming

By the early 1960's most computer manufacturers had two distinct, and totally incompatible, product lines. On the one hand there were the word–oriented, large–scale scientific computers, such as the 7094, which were used for normal numerical calculations in science and engineering. On the other hand, there was the character oriented, commercial computers, such as the 1401, which was widely used by the banks and insurance companies for sorting and printing. Developing and maintaining two completely different product lines was an expensive proposition for the manufactures. In addition, many new computer customers initially needed a small machine but later outgrew it and wanted a bigger machine that would run all their old programs, but faster. IBM attempted to solve both of these problems at a single stroke by introducing the system/360. The 360 was a series of software–compatible machines ranging from 1401–sized which was more powerful than the 7084. The machines differed only in price and performance. Since all the machines had the same architecture and instruction set, programs written for one machine could run on all the others, at least in theory. Furthermore, the 360 was designed to handle both scientific and commercial computing. Thus a single family of machines could satisfy the needs of all customers. In subsequent years, IBM has come out with compatible successors to the 360 line, using more modern technology, known as the 370, 4300, 3080 and 3090 series.

The Fourth Generation (1980–Present)

1) Personal Computers

With the development of LSI (large scale integration) circuits, chips containing thousands of transistors on a square centimetre of silicon, the age of the personal computer dawned. In terms of architecture, Personal computers (initially called Microcomputers) were not all that different from minicomputers of the PDP- 11 class, but in terms of price they certainly were different. Where the minicomputer made it possible for a department in a company or university to have its own computer, the microprocessor chip made it possible for a single individual to have his or her personal computers.

In 1974 when Intel came out with the 8080, the first general–purpose 8 bit CPU, it wanted an operating system for the 8080, in part to be able to list it. In 1977, Digital Research rewrote CP/M to make it suitable for running on the many microcomputers using the 8080, Zilog Z80 and other CPU chips. Many application problems were written to run on CP/M allowing it to completely dominate the world of micro computing for about 5 years.

In the early 1980's IBM designed the IBM PC and looked around for software to run on it. By the time, in 1983 the IBM PC/AT came out with the Intel 80286 CPU, MS- DOS was firmly entrenched and CP/M was on its last legs. MS-DOS was later widely used on the 80386 and 80486. Although the initial version of MS-DOS was family primitive, subsequent versions included more advanced features, including many taken from UNIX.

Linux is an open–source operating system enhanced and backed by thousands of programmer's World Wide Web. It is a multitasking; multiprocessing operating system designed originally the use on personal computer. The name "Linux" is derived from its inventor Linux Torvalds. Torvalds was a student at the University of Helsinki, Finland in early 1990s when he wrote the first version of an UNIX–like kernel us a toy project. He later posted the code on the internet and asked Programmers across the world to help him build it into a working system. The result was Linux. Torvalds holds the copyright but permits free distribution of source code. That is his overseas development of kernel and owns its trademark. When someone submits a change or a further enhancement, Torvalds and his core team of kernel developers review the merit of adding it to kernel source code. Some popular operating systems are UNIX, MS–DOS, Microsoft windows, Microsoft Windows NT, and Linux.

1.3.   Functionalities of OS

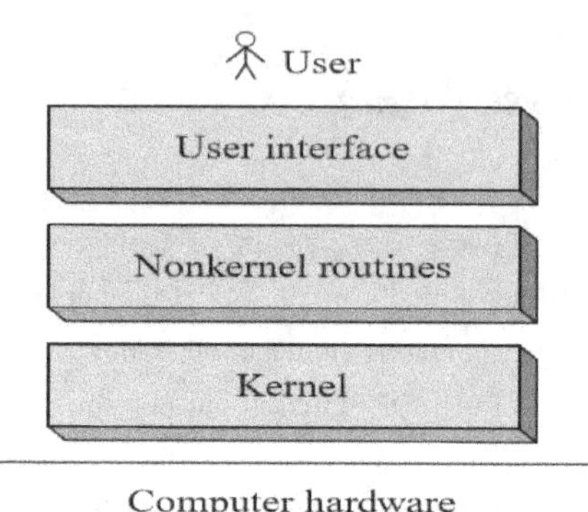

Figure 1.1: Abstract View of an OS

The typical functionalities of these parts are as follows:

- User interface: The user interface accepts commands to execute programs and use resources and services provided by the operating system. It is either a command line interface, as in Unix or Linux, which displays a command prompt to the user and accepts a user command, or is a graphical user interface (GUI), as in the Windows operating system, which interprets mouse clicks on icons as user commands.

- Nonkernel routines: These routines implement user commands concerning execution of programs and use of the computer's resources; they are invoked by the user interface.

- Kernel: The kernel is the core of the OS. It controls operation of the computer and provides a set of functions and services to use the CPU, memory, and other resources of the computer. The functions and services of the kernel are invoked by the nonkernel routines and by user programs.

Two features of an OS emerge from the designer's view of an OS shown in Figure 1.2. The OS is actually a collection of routines that facilitate execution of user programs and use of resources in a computer system. It contains a hierarchical arrangement of layers in which routines in a higher layer use the facilities provided by routines in the layer below it. In fact, each layer takes an abstract view of the layer below it, in which the next lower layer is a machine that can understand certain commands. The fact that the lower layer is a set of routines rather than a whole computer system makes no difference to the higher layer. Each higher layer acts as a more capable machine than the layer below it. To the user, the user interface appears like a machine that understands commands in the command language of the OS.

1.4. Key Benefits

Managing complexity: An abstract view of a system contains only selected features of the system. This property is useful in managing complexity during design or study of a system. For example, an abstract view of how an OS organizes execution of user programs (Figure 1.3 illustrates such a view later in this chapter), focuses only on handling of programs; it simplifies a study of this aspect of the OS by not showing how the OS handles other resources like memory or I/O devices.

Presenting a generic scheme: An abstraction is used to present a generic scheme that has many variants in practice. We see two examples of this use in the designer's abstract view of Figure 1.2. The user interface is an abstraction, with a command line interface and a graphical user interface (GUI) as two of its many variants. The kernel typically presents an abstraction of the computer system to the nonkernel routines so that the diversity of hardware, e.g., different models of CPUs and different ways of organizing and accessing data in disks, is hidden from view of the nonkernel routines.

1.5. Operation of an OS

The primary concerns of an OS during its operation are execution of programs, use of resources, and prevention of interference with programs and resources. Accordingly, its three principal functions are:

Program management: The OS initiates programs, arranges their execution on the CPU, and terminates them when they complete their execution. Since many programs exist in the system at any time, the OS performs a function called scheduling to select a program for execution.

Resource management: The OS allocates resources like memory and I/O devices when a program needs them. When the program terminates, it de-allocates these resources and allocates them to other programs that need them.

Security and protection: The OS implements non-interference in users' activities through joint actions of the security and protection functions. As an example, consider how the OS prevents illegal accesses to a file. The security function prevents nonusers from utilizing the services and resources in the computer system, hence none of them can access the file. The protection function prevents users other than the file owner or users authorized by him, from accessing the file.

When a computer system is switched on, it automatically loads a program stored on a reserved part of an I/O device, typically a disk, and starts executing the program. This program follows a software technique known as bootstrapping to load the software called the boot procedure in memory-the program initially loaded in memory loads some other programs in memory, which load other programs, and so on until the complete boot procedure is loaded. The boot procedure makes a list of all hardware resources in the system, and hands over control of the computer system to the OS.

A system administrator specifies which persons are registered as users of the system. The OS permits only these persons to log in to use its resources and services. A user authorizes his collaborators to access some programs and data. The OS notes this information and uses it to implement protection.

The OS also performs a set of functions to implement its notion of effective utilization. These functions include scheduling of programs and keeping track of resource status and resource usage information.

1.6.   Computer-System Architecture

In Section we introduced the general structure of a typical computer system. A computer system may be organized in a number of different ways, which we can categorize roughly according to the number of general-purpose processors used.

Single-Processor Systems

Most systems vise a single processor. The variety of single-processor systems may be surprising, however, since these systems range from PDAs through mainframes. On a single-processor system, there is one main CPU capable of executing a general-purpose instruction set, including instructions from user processes. Almost all systems have other special-purpose processors as well. They may come in the form of device-specific processors, such as disk, keyboard, and graphics controllers; or, on mainframes, they may come in the form of more general-purpose processors, such as I/O processors that move data rapidly among the components of the system. All of these special-purpose processors run a limited instruction set and do not run user processes. Sometimes they are managed by the operating system, in that the operating system sends them information about their next task and monitors their status. For example, a disk-controller microprocessor receives a sequence of requests from the main CPU and implements its own disk queue and scheduling algorithm. This arrangement relieves the main CPU of the overhead of disk scheduling. PCs contain a microprocessor in the keyboard to convert the keystrokes into codes to be sent to the CPU. In other systems or circumstances, special-purpose processors are low-level components built into the hardware. The operating system cannot communicate with these processors; they do their jobs autonomously. The use of special-purpose microprocessors is common and does not turn a single-processor system into a multiprocessor. If there is only one general-purpose CPU, then the system is a single-processor system.

Multiprocessor Systems

Although single-processor systems are most common, multiprocessor systems (also known as parallel systems or tightly coupled systems) are growing in importance. Such systems have two or more processors in close communication, sharing the computer bus and sometimes the clock, memory, and peripheral devices.

Multiprocessor systems have three main advantages:

- **Increased throughput:** By increasing the number of processors, we expect to get more work done in less time. The speed-up ratio with N processors is not N, however; rather, it is less than N. When multiple processors cooperate on a task, a certain amount of overhead is incurred in keeping all the parts working correctly. This overhead, plus contention for shared resources, lowers the expected gain from additional processors. Similarly, N programmers working closely together do not produce N times the amount of work a single programmer would produce.

- **Economy of scale:** Multiprocessor systems can cost less than equivalent multiple single-processor systems, because they can share peripherals, mass storage, and power supplies. If several programs operate on the same set of data, it is cheaper to store those data on one disk and to have all the processors share them than to have many computers with local disks and many copies of the data.

- **Increased reliability:** If functions can be distributed properly among several processors, then the failure of one processor will not halt the system, only slow it down. If we have ten processors and one fails, then each of the remaining nine processors can pick up a share of the work of the failed processor. Thus, the entire system runs only 10 percent slower, rather than failing altogether.

Increased reliability of a computer system is crucial in many applications. The ability to continue providing service proportional to the level of surviving hardware is called graceful degradation. Some systems go beyond graceful degradation and are called fault tolerant, because they can suffer a failure of any single component and still continue operation. Note that fault tolerance requires a mechanism to allow the failure to be detected, diagnosed, and, if possible, corrected. The HP Nonstop system (formerly Tandem) system uses both hardware and software duplication to ensure continued operation despite faults. The system consists of multiple pairs of CPUs, working in lockstep. Both processors in the pair execute each instruction and compare the results. If the results differ, then one CPU of the pair is at fault, and both are halted. The process that was being executed is then moved to another pair of CPUs, and the instruction that failed is restarted. This solution is expensive, since it involves special hardware and considerable hardware duplication.

The multiple-processor systems in use today are of two types. Some systems use asymmetric multiprocessing, in which each processor is assigned a specific task. A master processor controls the system; the other processors either look to the master for instruction or have predefined tasks. This scheme defines a master-slave relationship. The master processor schedules and allocates work to the slave processors.

The most common systems use symmetric multiprocessing (SMP), in which each processor performs all tasks within the operating system. SMP means that all processors are peers; no master-slave relationship exists between processors. Figure 1.2 illustrates a typical SMP architecture. An example of the SMP system is Solaris, a commercial version of UNIX designed by Sun Microsystems. A Solaris system can be configured to employ dozens of processors, all running Solaris.

The benefit of this model is that many processes can run simultaneously—N processes can run if there are N CPUs—without causing a significant deterioration of performance. However, we must carefully control I/O to ensure that the data reach the appropriate processor. Also, since the CPUs are separate, one may be sitting idle while another is overloaded, resulting in inefficiencies. These inefficiencies can be avoided if the processors share certain data structures. A multiprocessor system of this form will allow processes and resources—such as memory—to be shared dynamically among the various processors and can lower the variance among the processors. Such a system must be written carefully, as we shall see in Chapter 6. Virtually all modern operating systems—including Windows, Windows XP, Mac OS X, and Linux—now provide support for SMP.

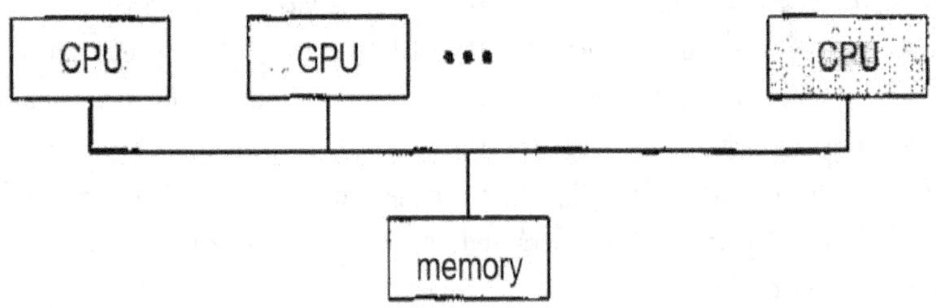

Figure 1.2: Symmetric Multiprocessing Architecture

The difference between symmetric and asymmetric multiprocessing may result from either hardware or software. Special hardware can differentiate the multiple processors, or the software can be written to allow only one master and multiple slaves. For instance, Sun's operating system SunOS Version 4 provided asymmetric multiprocessing, whereas Version 5 (Solaris) is symmetric on the same hardware.

A recent trend in CPU design is to include multiple compute cores on a single chip. In essence, these are multiprocessor chips. Two-way chips are becoming mainstream, while N-way chips are going to be common in high-end systems. Aside from architectural considerations such as cache, memory, and bus contention, these multi-core CPUs look to the operating system just as N standard processors.

Lastly, blade servers are a recent development in which multiple processor boards, I/O boards, and networking boards are placed in the same chassis. The difference between these and traditional multiprocessor systems is that each blade-processor board boots independently and runs its own operating system. Some blade-server boards are multiprocessor as well, which blurs the lines between types of computers. In essence, those servers consist of multiple independent multiprocessor systems.

Clustered Systems

Another type of multiple-CPU system is the clustered system. Like multiprocessor systems, clustered systems gather together multiple CPUs to accomplish computational work. Clustered systems differ from multiprocessor systems, however, in that they are composed of two or more individual systems coupled together. The definition of the term clustered is not concrete; many commercial packages wrestle with what a clustered system is and why one form is better than another. The generally accepted definition is that clustered computers share storage and are closely linked via a local-area network (LAN) or a faster interconnect such as InfiniBand.

Clustering is usually used to provide high-availability service; that is, service will continue even if one or more systems in the cluster fail. High availability is generally obtained by adding a level of redundancy in the system. A layer of cluster software runs on the cluster nodes. Each node can monitor one or more of the others (over the LAN). If the monitored machine fails, the monitoring machine can take ownership of its storage and restart the applications that were running on the failed machine. The users and clients of the applications see only a brief interruption of service.

Clustering can be structured asymmetrically or symmetrically. In asymmetric clustering, one machine is in hot-standby mode while the other is running the applications. The hot-standby host machine does nothing but monitor the active server. If that server fails, the hot-standby host becomes the active server. In symmetric mode, two or more hosts are running applications, and are monitoring each other. This mode is obviously more efficient, as it uses all of the available hardware. It does require that more than one application be available to run.

Other forms of clusters include parallel clusters and clustering over a wide-area network (WAN). Parallel clusters allow multiple hosts to access the same data on the shared storage. Because most operating systems lack support for simultaneous data access by multiple hosts, parallel clusters are usually accomplished by use of special versions of software and special releases of applications. For example, Oracle Parallel Server is a version of Oracle's database that has been designed to run on a parallel cluster. Each machine runs Oracle, and a layer of software tracks access to the shared disk. Each machine has full access to all data in the database. To provide this shared access to data, the system must also supply access control and locking to ensure that no conflicting operations occur. This function, commonly known as a distributed lock manager (DLM), is included in some cluster technology.

Cluster technology is changing rapidly. Some cluster products support dozens of systems in a cluster, as well as clustered nodes that are separated by miles. Many of these improvements are made possible by storage-area networks (SANs), which allow many systems to attach to a pool of storage.

If the applications and their data are stored on the SAN, then the cluster software can assign the application to run on any host that is attached to the SAN. If the host fails, then any other host can take over. In a database cluster, dozens of hosts can share the same database, greatly increasing performance and reliability.

1.7. Computer Hardware Review

Processors

The brain of the computer is the CPU. It fetches instructions from memory and executes them. The basic cycle of every CPU is to fetch the first instruction from memory, decode it to determine its type and operands, execute it, and the fetch, decode, and execute subsequent instructions. In this way, programs are carried out.

In addition to the general registers, which is used to hold variables and temporary results, most computers have several special registers that are visible to the programmer. One of these is the Program Counter, which contains the memory address of the next instruction to be fetched. After the instruction has been fetched, the program counter is updated to point to its successor.

Another register is the stack pointer which points to the top of the current stack in memory. The stack contains one frame for each procedure that has been entered but not yet exited.

Yet another register is the PSW (Program Status Word) this register contains the condition code bits, which are set by comparison instructions, the CPU priority, the mode and various other control bits. User programs may normally read the entire PSW but typically may write only some of its fields. The PSW plays an important role in system calls and I/O.

Memory

The second major component is any computer is the memory. Ideally, a memory should be extremely first, abundantly large, and dirt cheap. No current technology satisfies all of these goals, so a different approach is taken. The memory system is constructed as a hierarchy of layers as shown in the fig.

The top layer consists of the registers internal to the CPU. They are made of the same material as the CPU and are thus just as fast as the CPU. In this, memory is divided into several categories cache, RAM, ROM, EEPROM, and CMOs.

Cache memory, which is mostly controlled by the hardware. Main memory is divided up into cache lines typically 64 bytes, with addresses 0 to 63 in cache line 0, addresses 64 to 127 in cache line 1, and soon. When the program needs to read a memory word, the cache hardware checks to see of the line needed is in the cache. If needed it is, called a cache bit, the request is satisfied from the cache and no memory request is sent over the bust to the main memory. Cache memory is limited in size due to its high cost. Some machines have two or even three levels of cache, each on slower and bigger than the one before it.

RAM is a Random Access Memory; old timers sometimes call it Cory memory, because computers in the 1950's and 1960s used tiny magnetisable ferrite cores for main memory. Currently, memories are ten to hundreds of megabytes and growing rapidly. All CPU requests that cannot be satisfied out of the cache go to main memory.

ROM is a Read Only Memory, which is programmed at the factory and cannot be changed afterwards. It is fast and inexpensive. On some computers, the bootstrap loader used to start the computer is contained in ROM. Also, some I/O cards come with ROM for handling low – level device control.

EEPROM (Electrically Erasable ROM) and flash RAM are also non-volatile, but in contrast to ROM can be erased and rewritten. However, writing them takes orders of magnitude more time than writing RAM, so they are used in the same way ROM is, only with the additional feature that it is now possible to correct bugs in programs they hold by rewriting them in the field.

Yet another kind of memory is CMOS, which is volatile, many computers use CMOS memory to hold the current time and date. The CMOS memory and the check circuits that increments the time in it are powered by a small battery, so the time is correctly updated, even when the computer is unplugged.

I/O Devices

Memory is not the only resource that the operating system must manage I/O devices also interact heavily with the operating system. Normally I/O devices consist of two parts: a controllers and device itself. Controller is a chip or a set of chips on a plug–in board that physically controls the device. It accepts commands from the operating system, for example, to red data from the device, and carries them out. In many cases, the actual control of the device is very complicated and detailed, so it is the job of the controller to present a simpler interface to the operating system.

Controller is different software is needed to control each one. The software that talks to a controller, giving its commands and accepting responses, is called a device driver. Each controller manufacture has to supply a driver for each operating system is supports. Every controller has a small number of registers that are used to communicate with it. For example, a minimal disk controller might have register for specifying the disk address, memory address, sector count and direction. To activate the controller the driver gets a command from the operating system, then translates it into the appropriate values to write into the device registers.

Buses

Normally figure has eight buses (cache, local, memory, PCI, SCSI, USB, IDE and ISA). Each with a different transfer rate and function. The operating system must be aware of all of them for configuration and management. The two main buses are the original IBM PC ISA (Industry Standard Architecture) bus and its processor, (successor). The PCI (Peripheral Component Interconnect) bus. The ISA bus, which was originally the IBM PC/AT bus, run at 8.33 MHz and can transfer 2 bytes at once; for a maximum speed of 16.67 MB/sec.

In addition, this system contains three specialized buses: IDE, USB and SCSI. The IDE bus is for attaching peripheral devices such as disks and CD ROMs to the system. The IDE bus is an outgrowth of the disk controller interface on the PC/AT and is now standard on nearly all Pentium–based system for the hard disk and often the CD–ROM. The USB (Universal Serial Bus) was invented to attach all the slow I/O devices such as the keyboard and mouse, to the computer. It uses a small four wire connector, two of which supply electrical power to the USB devices. USB is a centralized bus in which a root device polls the I/O devices every 1 m sec to see if they have any traffic. The SCSI (Small computer System Interface) bus is a high–performance bus intended for fast disks, scanners and other devices needing considerable bandwidth. It can run at up to 160 MB/sec.

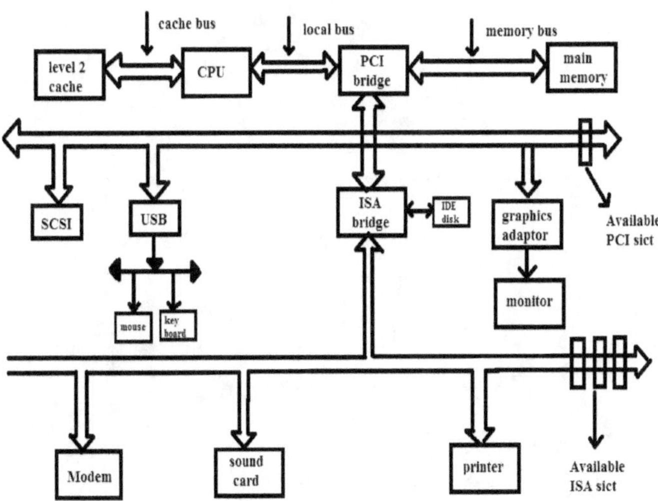

Figure 1.3: Structure of Large Pentium System

CHAPTER 2

PROCESS MANAGEMENT

A program does nothing unless its instructions are executed by a CPU. A program in execution, as mentioned, is a process. A time-shared user program such as a compiler is a process. A word-processing program being run by an individual user on a PC is a process. A system task, such as sending output to a printer, can also be a process (or at least part of one). For now, you can consider a process to be a job or a time-shared program, but later you will learn that the concept is more general. As we shall see in Chapter 3, it is possible to provide system calls that allow processes to create sub processes to execute concurrently.

A process needs certain resources including CPU time, memory, files, and I/O devices—to accomplish its task. These resources are either given to the process when it is created or allocated to it while it is running. In addition to the various physical and logical resources that a process obtains when it is created, various initialization data (input) may be passed along. For example, consider a process whose function is to display the status of a file on the screen of a terminal. The process will be given as an input the name of the file and will execute the appropriate instructions and system calls to obtain and display on the terminal the desired information. When the process terminates, the operating system will reclaim any reusable resources.

We emphasize that a program by itself is not a process; a program is a passive entity, such as the contents of a file stored on disk, whereas a process is an active entity. A single-threaded process has one program counter specifying the next instruction to execute. (Threads will be covered in Chapter 4.) The execution of such a process must be sequential. The CPU executes one instruction of the process after another, until the process completes. Further, at any time, one instruction at most is executed on behalf of the process. Thus, although two processes may be associated with the same program, they are nevertheless considered two separate execution sequences. A multithreaded process has multiple program counters, each pointing to the next instruction to execute for a given thread.

A process is the unit of work in a system. Such a system consists of a collection of processes, some of which are operating-system processes (those that execute system code) and the rest of which are user processes (those that execute user code). All these processes can potentially execute concurrently-by multiplexing the CPU among them on a single CPU, for example.

The operating system is responsible for the following activities in connection with process management:

- Creating and deleting both user and system processes
- Suspending and resuming processes
- Providing mechanisms for process synchronization
- Providing mechanisms for process communication
- Providing mechanisms for deadlock handling

2.1. Process Model

In this model, all the runnable software on the computer, sometimes including the operating system, is organized into a number of sequential processes, or just processes for short. A process is just an instance of an executing program, including the current values of the program counter, registers, and variables. Conceptually, each process has its own virtual CPU. In reality, of course, the real CPU switches back and forth from process to process, but to understand the system, it is much easier to think about a collection of processes running in (pseudo) parallel than to try to keep track of how the CPU switches from program to program. This rapid switching back and forth is called multiprogramming.

In Fig. 2.1(a) we see a computer multiprogramming four programs in memory. In Fig. 2.1(b) we see four processes, each with its own flow of control (i.e., its own logical program counter), and each one running independently of the other ones. Of course, there is only one physical program counter, so when each process runs, its logical program counter is loaded into the real program counter. When it is finished (for the time being), the physical program counter is saved in the process' stored logical program counter in memory. In Fig. 2.1(c) we see that viewed over a long enough time interval, all the processes have made progress, but at any given instant only one process is actually running.

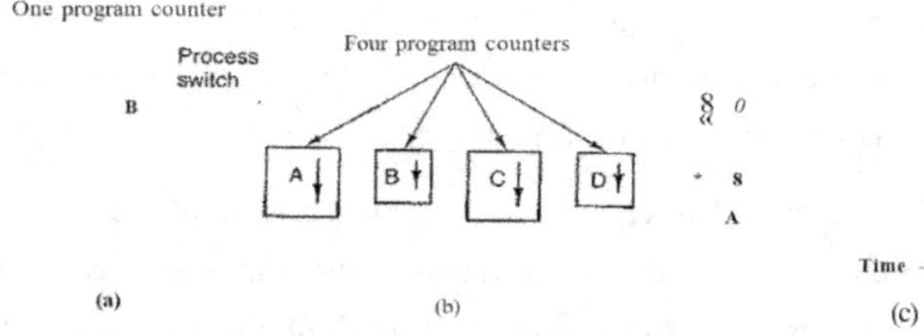

Figure 2.1: (a) Multiprogramming of Four Programs, (b) Conceptual Model of Four Independent, Sequential Processes, (c) Only One Program is Active at Once

In this chapter, we will assume there is only one CPU. Increasingly, however, that assumption is not true, since new chips are often multicore, with two, four, or more CPUs. We will look at multicore chips and multiprocessors in general in Chap. 8, but for the time being, it is simpler just to think of one CPU at a time. So when we say that a CPU can really only run one process at a time, if there are two cores (or CPUs) each one of them can run only one process at a time.

With the CPU switching rapidly back and forth among the processes, the rate at which a process performs its computation will not be uniform and probably not even reproducible if the same processes are run again. Thus, processes must not be programmed with built-in assumptions about timing. Consider, for example, an I/O process that starts a streamer tape to restore backed-up files, executes an idle loop 10,000 times to let it get up to speed, and then issues a command to read the first record. If the CPU decides to switch to another process during the idle loop, the tape process might not run again until after the first record was already past the read head. When a process has critical real-time requirements like this, that is, particular events must occur within a specified number of milliseconds, special measures must be taken to ensure that they do occur. Normally, however, most processes are not affected by the underlying multiprogramming of the CPU or the relative speeds of different processes.

The difference between a process and a program is subtle, but crucial. An analogy may help here. Consider a culinary-minded computer scientist who is baking a birthday cake for his daughter. He has a birthday cake recipe and a kitchen well stocked with all the input: flour, eggs, sugar, extract of vanilla, and so on. In this analogy, the recipe is the program (i.e., an algorithm expressed in some suitable notation), the computer scientist is the processor (CPU), and the cake ingredients are the input data. The process is the activity consisting of our baker reading the recipe, fetching the ingredients, and baking the cake.

Now imagine that the computer scientist's son comes running in screaming his head off, saying that he has been stung by a bee. The computer scientist records where he was in the recipe (the state of the current process is saved), gets out a first aid book, and begins following the directions in it. Here we see the processor being switched from one process (baking) to a higher-priority process (administering medical care), each having a different program (recipe versus first aid book). When the bee sting has been taken care of, the computer scientist goes back to his cake, continuing at the point where he left off. The key idea here is that a process is an activity of some kind. It has a program, input, output, and a state. A single processor may be shared among several processes, with some scheduling algorithm being used to determine when to stop work on one process and service a different one.

It is worth noting that if a program is running twice, it counts as two processes. For example, it is often possible to start a word processor twice or print two files at the same time if two printers are available. The fact that two running processes happen to be running the same program does not matter; they are distinct processes. The operating system may be able to share the code between them so only one copy is in memory, but that is a technical detail that does not change the conceptual situation of two processes running.

2.2.   Process Creation

Operating systems need some way to create processes. In very simple systems, or in systems designed for running only a single application (e.g., the controller in a microwave oven), it may be possible to have all the processes that will ever be needed be present when the system comes up. In general-purpose systems, however, some way is needed to create and terminate processes as needed during operation. We will now look at some of the issues.

There are four principal events that cause processes to be created:

- System initialization
- Execution of a process creation system call by a running process
- A user request to create a new process
- Initiation of a batch job

When an operating system is booted, typically several processes are created. Some of these are foreground processes, that is, processes that interact with (human) users and perform work for them. Others are background processes, which are not associated with particular users, but instead have some specific function. For example, one background process may be designed to accept incoming e-mail, sleeping most of the day but suddenly springing to life when incoming e-mail arrives. Another background process may be designed to accept incoming requests for Web pages hosted on that machine, waking up when a request arrives to service the request. Processes that stay in the background to handle some activity such as e-mail, Web pages, news, printing, and so on are called daemons. Large systems commonly have dozens of them. In UNIX, the ps program can be used to list the running processes. In Windows, the task manager can be used. In addition to the processes created at boot time, new processes can be created afterward as well. Often a running process will issue system calls to create one or more new processes to help it do its job. Creating new processes is particularly useful when the work to be done can easily be formulated in terms of several related, but otherwise independent interacting processes. For example, if a large amount of data is being fetched over a network for subsequent processing, it may be convenient to create one process to fetch the data and put them in a shared buffer while a second process removes the data items and processes them. On a multiprocessor, allowing each process to run on a different CPU may also make the job go faster.

In interactive systems, users can start a program by typing a command or (double) clicking an icon. Taking either of these actions starts a new process and runs the selected program in it. In command-based UNIX systems running X, the new process takes over the window in which it was started. In Microsoft Windows, when a process is started it does not have a window, but it can create one (or more) and most do. In both systems, users may have multiple windows open at once, each running some process. Using the mouse, the user can select a window and interact with the process, for example, providing input when needed.

The last situation in which processes are created applies only to the batch systems found on large mainframes. Here users can submit batch jobs to the system (possibly remotely). When the operating system decides that it has the resources to run another job, it creates a new process and runs the next job from the input queue in it.

Technically, in all these cases, a new process is created by having an existing process execute a process creation system call. That process may be a running user process, a system process invoked from the keyboard or mouse, or a batch manager process. What that process does is execute a system call to create the new process. This system call tells the operating system to create a new process and indicates, directly or indirectly, which program to run in it.

In UNIX, there is only one system call to create a new process: fork. This call creates an exact clone of the calling process. After the fork, the two processes, the parent and the child, have the same memory image, the same environment strings, and the same open files. That is all there is. Usually, the child process then executes execve or a similar system call to change its memory image and run a new program. For example, when a user types a command, say, sort, to the shell, the shell forks off a child process and the child executes sort. The reason for this two-step process is to allow the child to manipulate its file descriptors after the fork but before the execve in order to accomplish redirection of standard input, standard output, and standard error.

In Windows, in contrast, a single Win32 function call, Create Process, handles both process creation and loading the correct program into the new process. This call has 10 parameters, which include the program to be executed, the command-line parameters to feed that program, various security attributes, bits that control whether open files are inherited, priority information, a specification of the window to be created for the process (if any), and a pointer to a structure in which information about the newly created process is returned to the caller. In addition to Create Process, Win32 has about 100 other functions for managing and synchronizing processes and related topics.

In both UNIX and Windows, after a process is created, the parent and child have their own distinct address spaces. If either process changes a word in its address space, the change is not visible to the other process. In UNIX, the child's initial address space is a copy of the parent's, but there are definitely two distinct address spaces involved; no writable memory is shared (some UNIX implementations share the program text between the two since that cannot be modified). It is, however, possible for a newly created process to share some of its creator's other resources, such as open files. In Windows, the parent's and child's address spaces are different from the start.

2.3.   Process Termination

After a process has been created, it starts running and does whatever its job is. However, nothing lasts forever, not even processes.

Sooner or later the new process will terminate, usually due to one of the following conditions:

- Normal exit (voluntary)
- Error exit (voluntary)
- Fatal error (involuntary)
- Killed by another process (involuntary)

Most processes terminate because they have done their work. When a compiler has compiled the program given to it, the compiler executes a system call to tell the operating system that it is finished. This call is exit in UNIX and Exit Process in Windows. Screen-oriented programs also support voluntary termination. Word processors, Internet browsers and similar programs always have an icon or menu item that the user can click to tell the process to remove any temporary files it has open and then terminate.

The second reason for termination is that the process discovers a fatal error. For example, if a user types the command cc foo.c to compile the program foo.c and no such file exists, the compiler simply exits. Screen-oriented interactive processes generally do not exist when given bad parameters. Instead they pop up a dialog box and ask the user to try again. The third reason for termination is an error caused by the process, often due to a program bug. Examples include executing an illegal instruction, referencing nonexistent memory, or dividing by zero.

In some systems (e.g., UNIX), a process can tell the operating system that it wishes to handle certain errors itself, in which case the process is signalled (interrupted) instead of terminated when one of the errors occurs.

The fourth reason a process might terminate is that the process executes a system call telling the operating system to kill some other process. In UNIX this call is kill. The corresponding Win32 function is Terminate Process. In both cases, the killer must have the necessary .authorization to do in the killee. In some systems, when a process terminates, either voluntarily or otherwise, all processes it created are immediately killed as well. Neither UNIX nor Windows works this way, however.

2.4.   Process Hierarchies

In some systems, when a process creates another process, the parent process and child process continue to be associated in certain ways. The child process can itself create more processes, forming a process hierarchy. Note that unlike plants and animals that use sexual reproduction, a process has only one parent (but zero, one, two, or more children).

In UNIX, a process and all of its children and further descendants together form a process group. When a user sends a signal from the keyboard, the signal is delivered to all members of the process group currently associated with the keyboard (usually ail active processes that were created in the current window). Individually, each process can catch the signal, ignore the signal, or take the default action, which is to be killed by the signal.

As another example of where the process hierarchy plays a role, let us look at how UNIX initializes itself when it is started. A special process, called init, is present in the boot image. When it starts running, it reads a file telling how many terminals there are. Then it forks off one new process per terminal. These processes wait for someone to log in.

If a login is successful, the login process executes a shell to accept commands. These commands may start up more processes, and so forth. Thus, all the processes in the whole system belong to a single tree, with init at the root.

In contrast, Windows has no concept of a process hierarchy. All processes are equal. The only hint of a process hierarchy is that when a process is created, the parent is given a special token (called a handle) that it can use to control the child. However, it is free to pass this token to some other process, thus invalidating the hierarchy. Processes in UNIX cannot disinherit their children.

2.5.   Process States

Although each process is an independent entity, with its own program counter and internal state, processes often need to interact with other processes. One process may generate some output that another process uses as input. In the shell command cat chapter 1 chapter 2 chapters | grep tree.

The first process, running cat, concatenates and outputs three files. The second process, running grep, selects all lines containing the word "tree." Depending on the relative speeds of the two processes (which depends on both the relative complexity of the programs and how much CPU time each one has had), it may happen that grep is ready to run, but there is no input waiting for it. It must then block until some input is available.

When a process blocks, it does so because logically it cannot continue, typically because it is waiting for input that is not yet available. It is also possible for a process that is conceptually ready and able to run to be stopped because the operating system has decided to allocate the CPU to another process for a while. These two conditions are completely different. In the first case, the suspension is inherent in the problem (you cannot process the user's command line until it has been typed). In the second case, it is a technicality of the system (not enough CPUs to give each process its own private processor). In Figure 2.2 we see a state diagram showing the three states a process may be in:

- Running (actually using the CPU at that instant)
- Ready (runnable; temporarily stopped to let another process run)
- Blocked (unable to run until some external event happens)

Logically, the first two states are similar. In both cases the process is willing to run, only in the second one, there is temporarily no CPU available for it. The third state is different from the first two in that the process cannot run, even if the CPU has nothing else to do.

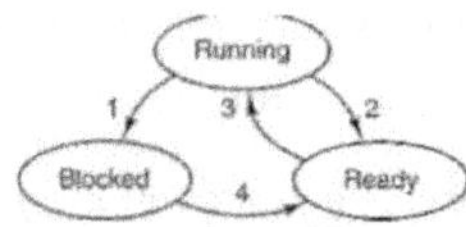

1. Process Blocks for Input | 2. Scheduler Picks Another Process

3. Scheduler Picks this Process | 4. Input Becomes Available

Figure 2.2: A Process can be in Running, Blocked, or Ready State. Transitions between these States are as Shown

Four transitions are possible among these three states, as shown. Transition 1 occurs when the operating system discovers that a process cannot continue right now. In some systems the process can execute a system call, such as pause, to get into blocked state. In other systems, including UNDC, when a process reads from a pipe or special file (e.g., a terminal) and there is no input available, the process is automatically blocked.

Transitions 2 and 3 are caused by the process scheduler, a part of the operating system, without. The process even knowing about them. Transition 2 occurs when the scheduler decides that the running process has run long enough, and it is time to let another process have some CPU time. Transition 3 occurs when all the other processes have had their fair share and it is time for the first process to get the CPU to run again.

The subject of scheduling, that is, deciding which process should run when and for how long, is an important one; we will look at it later in this chapter. Many algorithms have been devised to try to balance the competing demands of efficiency for the system as a whole and fairness to individual processes. We will study some of them later in this chapter.

Transition 4 occurs when the external event for which a process was waiting (such as the arrival of some input) happens. If no other process is running at that instant, transition 3 will be triggered and the process will start running. Otherwise it may have to wait in ready state for a little while until the CPU is available and its turn comes.

Using the process model, it becomes much easier to think about what is going on inside the system. Some of the processes run programs that carry «out commands typed in by a user. Other processes are part of the system and handle tasks such as carrying out requests for file services or managing the details of running a disk or a tape drive. When a disk interrupt occurs, the system makes a decision to stop running the current process and run the disk process, which was blocked waiting for that interrupt. Thus, instead of thinking about interrupts, we can think about user processes, disk processes, terminal processes, and so on, which block when they are waiting for something to happen. When the disk has been read or the character typed, the process waiting for it is unblocked and is eligible to run again.

This view gives rise to the model shown in Figure 2.3. Here the lowest level of the operating system is the scheduler, with a variety of processes on top of it. All the interrupt handling and details of actually starting and stopping processes are hidden away in what is here called the scheduler, which is actually not much code. The rest of the operating system is nicely structured in process form. Few real systems are as nicely structured as this, however.

2.6.   Implementation of Processes

To implement the process model, the operating system maintains a table (an array of structures), called the process table, with one entry per process. (Some authors call these entries process control blocks.) This entry contains important information about the process' state, including its program counter, stack pointer, memory allocation, the status of its open files, its accounting and scheduling information, and everything else about the process that must be saved when the process is switched from running to ready or blocked state so that it can be restarted later as if it had never been stopped.

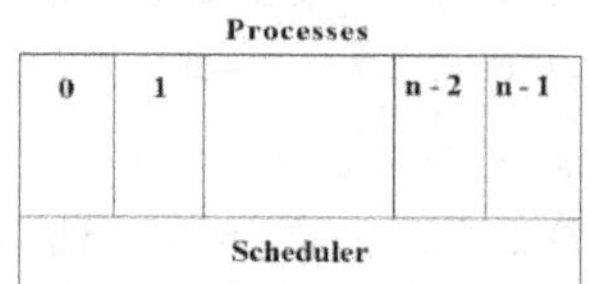

Figure 2.3: The Lowest Layer of a Process-structured Operating System Handles Interrupts and Scheduling. Above that Layer are Sequential Processes

Figure 2.4 shows some of the key fields in a typical system. The fields in the first column relate to process management. The other two relate to memory management and file management, respectively. It should be noted that precisely which fields the process table has is highly system dependent, but this figure gives a general idea of the kinds of information needed.

Process management	Memory management	File management
Registers	Pointer to text segment info	Root directory
Program counter	Pointer to data segment info	Working directory
Program status word	Pointer to stack segment info	File descriptors
Stack pointer		User ID
Process state		Group ID
Priority		
Scheduling parameters		
Process ID		
Parent process		
Process group		
Signals		
Time when process started		
CPU time used		
Children's CPU time		
Time of next alarm		

Figure 2.4: Some of the Fields of a Typical Process Table Entry

Now that we have looked at the process table, it is possible to explain a little more about how the illusion of multiple sequential processes is maintained on one (or each) CPU. Associated with each I/O class is a location (typically at a fixed location near the bottom of memory) called the interrupt vector. It contains the address of the interrupt service procedure. Suppose that user process 3 is running when a disk interrupt happens. User process 3's program counter, program status word, and sometimes one or more registers are pushed onto the (current) stack by the interrupt hardware. The computer then jumps to the address specified in the interrupt vector. That is all the hardware does. From here on, it is up to the software, in particular, the interrupt service procedure.

All interrupts start by saving the registers, often in the process table entry for the current process. Then the information pushed onto the stack by the interrupt is removed and the stack pointer is set to point to a temporary stack used by the process handler. Actions such as saving the registers and setting the stack pointer cannot even be expressed in high-level languages such as C, so they are performed by a small assembly language routine, usually the same one for all interrupts since the work of saving the registers is identical, no matter what the cause of the interrupt is.

When this routine is finished, it calls a C procedure to do the rest of the work for this specific interrupt type. (We assume the operating system is written in C, the usual choice for all real operating systems.) When it has done its job, possibly making some process now ready, the scheduler is called to see who to run next. After that, control is passed back to the assembly language code to load up the registers and memory map for the now-current process and start it running. Interrupt handling and scheduling are summarized AS,

- Hardware stacks program counter, etc.
- Hardware loads new program counter from interrupt vector.
- Assembly language procedure saves registers.
- Assembly language procedure sets up new stack.
- C interrupt service runs {typically reads and buffers input).
- Scheduler decides which process is to run next.
- C procedure returns to the assembly code.
- Assembly language procedure starts up new current process.

It is worth noting that the details vary somewhat from system to system. When the process finishes, the operating system displays a prompt character and waits for a new command. When it receives the command, it loads a new program into memory, overwriting the first one.

2.7.   Modeling Multiprogramming

When multiprogramming is used, the CPU utilization can be improved. Crudely put, if the average process computes only 20% of the time it is sitting in memory, with five processes in memory at once, the CPU should be busy all the time. This model is unrealistically optimistic, however, since it tacitly assumes that all five processes will never be waiting for I/O at the same time. A better model is to look at CPU usage from a probabilistic viewpoint. Suppose that a process spends a fraction p of its time waiting for I/O to complete. With n processes in memory at once, the probability that all n processes are waiting for I/O (in which case the CPU will be idle) is p". The CPU utilization is then given by the formula

$$\text{CPU utilization} \sim \backslash\text{-p"}$$

Figure 2.5 shows the CPU utilization as a function of n, which is called the degree of multiprogramming.

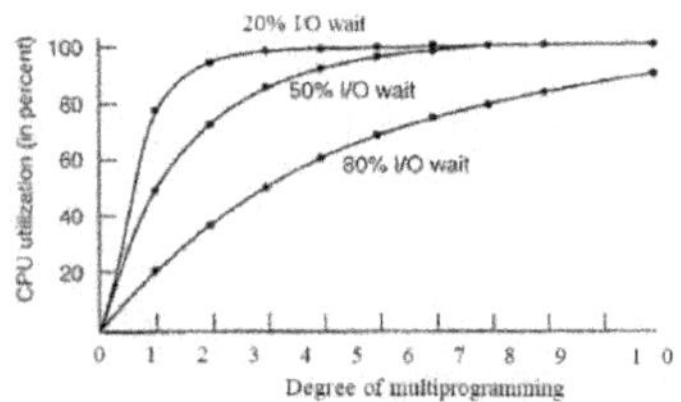

Figure 2.5: CPU Utilization as a Function of the Number of Processes in Memory

From the figure it is clear that if processes spend 80% of their time waiting for I/O, at least 10 processes must be in memory at once to get the CPU waste below 10%. When you realize that an interactive process waiting for a user to type something at a terminal is in I/O wait state, it should be clear that I/O wait times of 80% and more are not unusual. But even on servers, processes doing a lot of disk I/O will often have this percentage or more.

For the sake of complete accuracy, it should be pointed out that the probabilistic model just described is only an approximation. It implicitly assumes that all n processes are independent, meaning that it is quite acceptable for a system with five processes in memory to have three running and two waiting. But with a single CPU, we cannot have three processes running at once, so a process becoming ready while the CPU is busy will have to wait. Thus the processes are not independent. A more accurate model can be constructed using queuing theory, but the point we are making—multiprogramming lets processes use the CPU when it would otherwise become idle—is, of course, still valid, even if the true curves of Fig. 2.5 are slightly different from those shown in the figure.

Even though the model of Figure 2.5 is simple-minded, it can nevertheless be used to make specific, although approximate, predictions about CPU performance. Suppose, for example, that a computer has 512 MB of memory, with the operating system taking up 128 MB and each user program also taking up 128 MB. These sizes allow three user programs to be in memory at once. With an 80% average I/O wait, we have a CPU utilization (ignoring operating system overhead) of 1 - 0.8³ or about 49%. Adding another 512 MB of memory allows the system to go from three-way multiprogramming to seven-way multiprogramming, thus raising the CPU utilization to 79%. In other words, the additional 512 MB will raise the throughput by 30%.

Adding yet another 512 MB would only increase CPU utilization from 79% to 91%, thus raising the throughput by only another 12%. Using this model the computer's owner might decide that the first addition is a good investment but that the second is not.

2.8.   Threads

A thread is a basic limit of execution. a thread is a single sequential flow of control within a program. A thread is also known as a light weight process. A process can have May threads of execution.

What Structure Does the Threads Have?

Recall that a process is a program in execution and the process structure is divided into code region, data region and stack region. The code region and data region of a process are shared across different threads of the same process (Refer to figure).

Each thread of a process has its own stack region and PC.

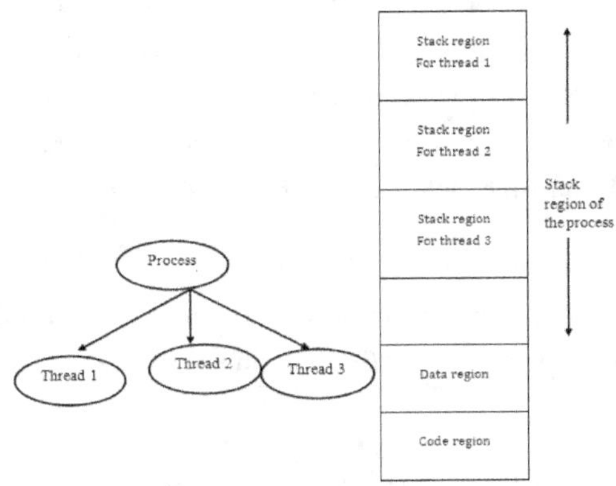

Figure 2.6: Thread Structure

Why is there a Need for Multiple Threads in a Process?

Consider the following real world example of a editing a document using an editor. This editing would be executed as a thread in the process. Suppose that the user also wants to use the spell check facility available with the editor. If the OS allows only one thread for each process (Single threading) then the user should first finish editing the document and then use the spell check facility. This would be time consuming and also during ht course of editing the CPU could be idle most of the times. Allowing multiple threads to executes concurrently in the case would improve the CPU utilization and also the spell check can be done as and when the document is edited. Figure indicates(illustrates).

Multithreading concept in the word editor. The spell checked runs consequently as and when the user edits the document. Another good example for multithreading would be the web browsers. As the browser fetches a document it will also concurrently allow the user to interact with the existing information in the browser.

Advantages of Multithreading

1) Multiple threads in a process share the same memory address space. This means memory utilization would be bettered by using multithreading.
2) Concurrent execution of threads would result in faster execution of the process.

2.9. Scheduling

The basis for multitasking is scheduling. Determining when a process is to be run, with in a multitasking environment is called scheduling. When a computer is multi programmed, it frequently has multiple processes competing for the CPU at the same time. This situation occurs whenever two or more processes are simultaneously in the state. If only one CPU is available, a choice has to be made which process to run next. The part of the operating system that makes the choice is called the scheduler and the algorithm it uses is called the scheduling algorithm. These topics form the subject matter of the following sections.

CPU Utilization

This gives a measure of what percentage of the CPU is being utilized. A scheduling algorithm should be chosen such that the CPU utilization is high.

Throughput

This measure indicates the number of processer executed per unit of time. A good scheduling algorithm is one which has a higher throughput.

Turnaround Time

This is a measure which gives the amount of time taken by a process for its execution. This includes the time spend by the process waiting for main memory, time spend waiting in the ready queue, time spend in executing on the CPU and the time spend doing an I/O. A good scheduling algorithm is one which has a lesser turnaround time for processes.

Waiting Time

This is a measure which gives the amount of time spent by the process waiting in the ready queue. This measure does not take into account the time spend in I/O. A good scheduling algorithm is one which reduces the waiting time for a process.

Response Time

The time taken for submission of a process until the first response is called response time. This measure is very useful in interactive computer systems. A good scheduling is algorithm is one where the response time for each process is as least as possible.

2.10. Types of Scheduling

Non-Preemptive Scheduling

In non-preemptive scheduling, a process which is allocated to the CPU time will continue to run until it terminates or until it gets blocked due to an I/O request. In this the scheduling process cannot be force dot relinquish the CPU time. An example of non-preemptive scheduling is the First Come First Serve(FCFS) scheduling policy. Here the process is allotted to the CPU time based on the order in which it enters the ready queue. An example of FCFS is the railway reservation counter.

One of the main disadvantages of the FCFS scheduling algorithm is the monopoly of a process. This could mean that a single process might take all of the CPU time without rehnquishing the same. In the railway reservation counter example this would mean that the current person who is booking the ticket might take most of the time of the reservation clerk by enquiring about various trains their availability. Consider the following illustration for FCFS scheduling policy.

Table 2.1: Illustration for FCFS Scheduling Algorithm

Process	Estimate runtime (in milliseconds)
P1	6
P2	8
P3	7
P4	3

Table shows four process (P1, P2, P3, P4) waiting in the ready queue for the execution. These processes would be executed in the order in which they entered the ready queue.(ie) P1 followed by P2 followed by P3 followed by P4 as shown in the Gantt chart(fig).

To find out the efficiency of the FCFS scheduling algorithm, the average waiting time is calculated.

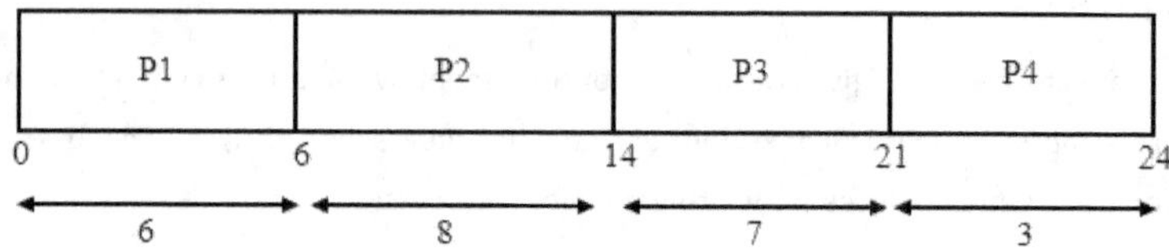

Figure 2.7: Gantt Chart for FCFS

The waiting time for P1=0 milliseconds (P1 starts executing first)

The waiting time for P2=6 milliseconds (P2 starts executing after 1)

The waiting time for P3=14 milliseconds (P3 starts executing after P1 and P2)

The waiting time for P4=21 milliseconds (P4 starts executing after P1,P2 and P3)

Hence the average waiting time= (0+6+14+21)/4 = 41/4= 10.25 milliseconds

Turn Around time (TAT) for P1 is=6, P2=14, P3=21, P4=24. Hence the average TAT is= 65/4= 16.25.

The average response time can be calculated as follows : Response time for P1=0, P2=6, P3=14, P4=21. Hence average response time is equal to 10.25 milliseconds. Average Turn Around time can also be calculated as average waiting time + average execution time. So in this example the average waiting time = 7ms and the average execution time = 24/6= 6; Hence average TAT=13ms.

Preemptive Scheduling

In preemptive scheduling the process which is currently running can be removed from the running state by the scheduler, in order to allow another process to run. This act of the scheduler is pre-emption. One mechanism of preemptive scheduling would be to specify a fixed time slice during which a process gets CPU time. If the time slice in 4ms and a process gets its time slice, then another process is given the CPU time. If the original process terminates before 4ms then the CPU will immediately take a context switch which ensures that another process is given the CPU time.

Shortest Job First(SJF) Algorithm Time

The SJF algorithm schedules the processes based on their given estimated run time. The process with the shortest estimated run time would be scheduled first followed by the next shortest and soon. The following real world example (Refer to figure) would help in better understanding of the SJF algorithm.

Consider the scenario where in water needs to be filled in a glass and a bucket from a single tap. Since the glass is of smaller size the water would be filled in the glass first and then followed by the bucket. This is nothing but shortest job first execution. Water from the tap is similar to the CPU and the act of filling in water into the glass and bucket are similar to two different processes. Consider the following illustration for SJF algorithm.

Table 2.2: Illustration for SJF Algorithm

Process	Estimated runtime in milliseconds
P1	6
P2	8
P3	7
P4	3

The above table shows for process(P1,P2,P3 and P4) waiting in the ready queue for the execution these processes would be executed based on their estimated run time. The process with the least estimated run time requirement would be executed first followed by the next least and soon. I-e P4 followed by P1 followed by P3 followed by P2 as shown in the Gantt chart in

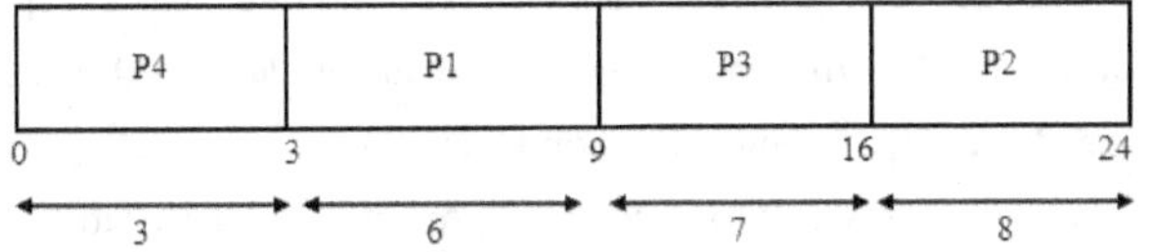

Figure 2.8: Gantt Chart for SJF Example

The average waiting time for the four processes when the SJF algorithm is used is calculated as follows:

The waiting for P4=o milliseconds (P4 starts executing first)

The waiting time for P1=3 milliseconds (P1 starts executing after P4)

The waiting time for P3=9 milliseconds (P3 starts executing after P4 and P1)

The waiting time for P2=16 milliseconds (P2 starts executing after P4, P1 and P3)

Hence the average waiting time   = (0+3+9+16)/4

= 28/4 = 7 milliseconds

Accordingly the average TAT will be 52/4=13 milliseconds(better than FCFS)

Average response time is calculated as follows:

P1=3; P4=0; P3=9;P2=16.

Hence average response time = 28/4= 7 milliseconds, which is much better than FCFS. In general SJF scheduling algorithm is better than FCFS scheduling algorithm as the average waiting time is less for SJF scheduling algorithm. The key point to note in SJF scheduling algorithm is that by moving the shorter process before a longer process. The waiting time of the shorter process decreases more than the increase in the waiting time for the longer process.

What if a new process (P5 with CPU time as 2ms) arrives into the ready queue when P1 which is currently being executed using the SJF scheduling algorithm has finished 1ms it CPU time i-e at 4th instance of time.

The SJF scheduling algorithm could either be preemptive or non-preemptive scheduling algorithm. If SJF scheduling algorithm is non-preemptive then as soon as P1 terminates P5 is scheduled.

Normally there are two categories of jobs that get into the ready queue. First category is that of the CPU sound jobs and the other category is that of the I/O bound jobs. CPU bound jobs are those which take a lot of CPU time but spend very less time in doing the I/O operations. On the other hand I/O bound jobs are those which take very less CPU time, but spend a lot of time doing I/O operations like printing, receiving input from the keyboard etc. if there are two processes in the ready queue, one being CPU bound and the other one being I/O bound, the I/O bound process which takes less CPU time could be preferred to be executed first and released to do its I/O operation.

This would result is lesser average waiting time. If SJF scheduling algorithm is preemptive then the scheduler checks whether the CPU time of P5 is shorter than what is the remaining of the total estimated time of the currently executing process P1. P1 has still 5ms of CPU time left over. Since P5's CPU time is shorter P1 is pre-empted before it could complete its execution and P5 is executed as shown in figure.

In such case, the average waiting time would become

(0+3+0+2+11+18)/5=34/5=6.5 ms

Whereas average turnaround time would be

$$(3+(6-4)+11+18+26/5=60/5=12 \text{ ms}$$

Preemptive SJF scheduling algorithm is also called as shortest remaining scheduling (SRT) algorithm.

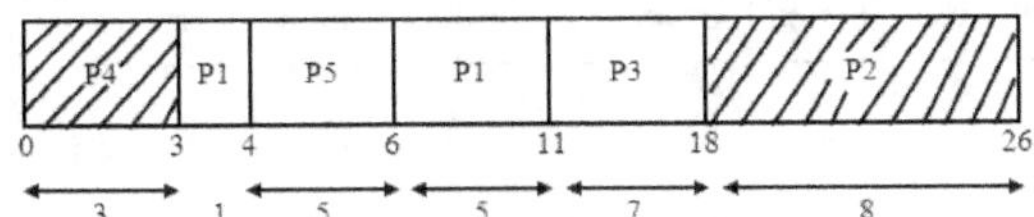

Figure 2.9: SJF Scheduling Algorithm

The main disadvantage of SJF scheduling algorithm is that more often it is difficult to know the next shortest process in the ready queue, as new processes keep entering the ready queue. also process which requires more CPU time may never get the CPU at all. This is called as starvation or live lock. In the above example, if more and more processes of time duration almost equal to P5 keep entering the ready queue. Then the processes P3,P4 may never get a chance to get executed by the CPU.

Round Robin(RR) Algorithm

The RR algorithm is primarily designed for operating systems where multiple users use the CPU time in such a way that every users feels that they have the whole computer for themselves. Such systems are called time sharing systems. The RR scheduling algorithm is similar to FCFS scheduling algorithm, except for the fact that the pre-emption is added to switch between the processes. In this scheme, a time slice is defined the ready queue is considered to be a circular queue. The scheduler goes around the ready queue, allocating the CPU to each process for a time interval up to 1 time slice.

Recall that a queue works on the principle of First in First Out (FIFO). New processes are added to the other end of the ready queue. The scheduler picks the first process from the read queue and schedules it for execution.

Now If the process terminates before the elapse of the time slice, then the process itself will release the CPU voluntarily. The scheduler will now proceed to next process in the ready queue. On the contrary if the process does not finish to execution during its allotted time slice then a context switch is done by the OS and the next process in the ready queue will be executed. This incomplete process which was pre-empted would be put at the other end of the queue. The advantage of RR scheduling algorithm is that it ensures every process gets a fixed amount of

CPU time unlike FCFS algorithm where there could be process waiting for CPU time for quite a long time. Calculate the average waiting time with respect to Round Robin scheduling with time slice=3 for the processes as shown in

Table 2.3: Process to be Scheduled

Process	Estimated runtime (in milliseconds)	Arrival time
P1	12	0
P2	10	0
P3	4	1
P4	10	4
P5	12	2

Solution

Refer figure The Average waiting time is calculated as follows:

Waiting time for P1   = 0+(15-3)+(28-18)+(40-31) = 31

P1	P2	P3	P5	P4	P1	P2	P3	P5	P4	P1	P2	P5	P4	P1	P2	P5	P4

Figure 2.10: Gantt Chart for Round Robin Scheduling

Waiting time for P2   =   3+(18-6)+(31-21)+(43-34)

                  =   34

Waiting time for P3   =   (6-1)+(21-9)

                  =   17

Waiting time for P4   =   (12-4)+(25-15)+(37-28)+(47-40)

                  =   34

Waiting time for P5   =   (9-2)+(22-12)+(34-25)+(44-37)

                  =   33

Hence average waiting time is equal to (31+34+17+34+33)/5=29.8 milliseconds. Note that P3 arrives at instance 1. Accordingly for the first slice the waiting time is (b-1). The rest of the calculation is self-explanatory. Calculating the average turnaround time and response time is left as an exercise. The disadvantage of RR scheduling algorithm is the overhead involved in maintaining the time slice information for every process which is currently being executed.

Priority Scheduling

In priority scheduling, each process is assigned a priority number which indicates the rating of these processes when compared to each other. This number is used in deciding which process should be scheduled. Consider the following real world examples of vehicles moving in a road(refer to figure) compared to other vehicles on the road an ambulance has a higher priority. Whenever an ambulance comes on a road all other vehicles need to give way for the ambulance because of its higher priority. Similarly in priority scheduling the process with the highest priority is selected for execution. Priority scheduling can be either preemptive or non-preemptive.

In preemptive priority scheduling whenever a higher priority process arrives the currently executing process is pre-empted and the new process is assigned to the CPU time. The ambulance example mentioned. In figure is an example for pre-emptive priority scheduling. Calculated the Average waiting time with respect to priority based preemptive scheduling (Assume priority 0 is greater than 1). In case of any tie, use FCFS.

Table 2.4: Process to be Scheduled

Process	Estimated machine(in milliseconds)	Arrival time	Priority
P1	12	0	2
P2	10	0	1
P3	4	1	0
P4	10	4	2
P5	12	2	1

Average waiting time = 14 Refer Figure for explanation.

The Average Waiting time= (26+(0+4)+0+(38-4)+(14-2))/5=76/5=15.2 milliseconds and the turnaround time will be=24.8 milliseconds

| 0 | 1 | 5 | 14 | 26 | 38 | 48 |

Figure 2.11: Gantt chart for Priority Based Preemptive Scheduling

In a non-preemptive priority scheduling the current executing process is not disturbed whenever a new higher priority process arrives. This higher priority process is placed at the beginning of the ready queue so that it could be scheduled for execution as soon as the currently execution process terminates.

Disadvantage

The main disadvantage in priority scheduling is that it can cause a lower priority process to wait in the ready queue for an indefinite time hence cawing starvation. One solution to this problem is to slowly increase the priority of a process which is waiting in the ready queue for a longer time. This will ensure that the low priority process will also eventually get executed as its priority would increase gradually. This technique increase the priority of processes which is waiting in the ready queue for a long time called aging.

2.11. Research on Processes and Threads

The concept of a process is an example of something that is fairly well settled. Almost every system has some notion of a process as a container for grouping together related resources such as an address space, threads, open files, protection permissions, and so on. Different systems do the grouping slightly differently, but these are just engineering differences. The basic idea is not very controversial any more, and there is little new research on the subject of processes.

Threads are a newer idea than processes, but they, too, have been chewed over quite a bit. Still, the occasional paper about threads appears from time to time, for example, about thread clustering on multiprocessors (Tarn et al., 2007) or scaling the number of threads in a process to 100,000 (Von Behren et al., 2003).

Process synchronization is pretty much cut and dried by now, but there is still a paper once in a while, such as one on concurrent processing without locks (Fraser and Harris, 2007) or nonblocking synchronization in real-time systems (Hohmuth and Haertig, 2001)

Scheduling (both uniprocessor and multiprocessor) is still a topic near and dear to the heart of some researchers. Some topics being researched include energy-efficient scheduling on mobile devices (Yuan and Nahrstedt, 2006), hyperthreading-aware scheduling (Bulpin and Pratt, 2005), what to do when the CPU would otherwise be idle (Eggert and Touch, 2005), and virtual-time scheduling (Nieh et al., 2001). However, few actual system designers are walking around all day wringing their hands for lack of a decent thread-scheduling algorithm, so it appears that this type of research is more researcher-push than demand-pull. All in all, processes, threads, and scheduling are not hot topics for research as they once were. The research has moved on.

2.12. Threading Issues

In this section, we discuss some of the issues to consider with multithreaded programs.

The fork() and exec() System Calls

If one thread in a program calls f ork(), does the new process duplicate all threads, or is the new process single-threaded? Some UNIX systems have chosen to have two versions of forkQ, one that duplicates all threads and another that duplicates only the thread that invoked the forkO system call. If a thread invokes the exec () system call, the program specified in the parameter to exec () will replace the entire process—including all threads. Which of the two versions of f orkO to use depends on the application. If execO is called immediately after forking, then duplicating all threads is unnecessary, as the program specified in the parameters to exec() will replace the process. In this instance, duplicating only the calling thread is appropriate. If, however, the separate process does not call exec() after forking, the separate process should duplicate all threads.

Cancellation

Thread cancellation is the task of terminating a thread before it has completed. For example, if multiple threads are concurrently searching through a database and one thread returns the result, the remaining threads might be canceled. Another situation might occur when a user presses a button on a web browser that stops a web page from loading any further. Often, a web page is loaded using several threads—each image is loaded in a separate thread. When a user presses the stop button on the browser, all threads loading the page are canceled. A thread that is to be canceled is often referred to as the target thread. Cancellation of a target thread may occur in two different scenarios:

- **Asynchronous cancellation**: One thread immediately terminates the target thread.
- **Deferred cancellation**: The target thread periodically checks whether it should terminate, allowing it an opportunity to terminate itself in an orderly fashion.

The difficulty with cancellation occurs in situations where resources have been allocated to a canceled thread or where a thread is canceled while in the midst of updating data it is sharing with other threads. This becomes especially troublesome with asynchronous cancellation. Often, the operating system will reclaim system resources from a canceled thread but will not reclaim all resources. Therefore, canceling a thread asynchronously may not free a necessary system-wide resource.

With deferred cancellation, in contrast, one thread indicates that a target thread is to be canceled, but cancellation occurs only after the target thread has checked a flag to determine if it should be canceled or not. This allows a thread to check whether it should be canceled at a point when it can be canceled safely. Pthreads refers to such points as cancellation points.

Signal Handling

A signal is used in UNIX systems to notify a process that a particular event has occurred. A signal may be received either synchronously or asynchronously, depending on the source of and the reason for the event being signaled. All signals, whether synchronous or asynchronous, follow the same pattern:

- A signal is generated by the occurrence of a particular event.
- A generated signal is delivered to a process.

- Once delivered, the signal must be handled.

Examples of synchronous signals include illegal memory access and division by 0. If a running program performs either of these actions, a signal is generated. Synchronous signals are delivered to the same process that performed the operation that caused the signal (that is the reason they are considered synchronous).

When a signal is generated by an event external to a running process, that process receives the signal asynchronously. Examples of such signals include terminating a process with specific keystrokes (such as <control><C>) and having a timer expire. Typically, an asynchronous signal is sent to another process. Every signal may be handled by one of two possible handlers:

- A default signal handler
- A user-defined signal handler

Every signal has a default signal handler that is run by the kernel when handling that signal. This default action can be overridden by a user-defined signal handler that is called to handle the signal. Signals may be handled in different ways. Some signals (such as changing the size of a window) may simply be ignored; others (such as an illegal memory access) may be handled by terminating the program. Handling signals in single-threaded programs is straightforward; signals are always delivered to a process. However, delivering signals is more complicated in multithreaded programs, where a process may have several threads. Where, then, should a signal be delivered? In general, the following options exist:

- Deliver the signal to the thread to which the signal applies.
- Deliver the signal to every thread in the process.
- Deliver the signal to certain threads in the process.
- Assign a specific thread to receive all signals for the process.

The method for delivering a signal depends on the type of signal generated. For example, synchronous signals need to be delivered to the thread causing the signal and not to other threads in the process. However, the situation with asynchronous signals is not as clear. Some asynchronous signals-such as a signal that terminates a process (<control><C>, for example) -should be sent to all threads. Most multithreaded versions of UNIX allow a thread to specify which signals it will accept and which it will block. Therefore, in some cases, an asynchronous signal may be delivered only to those threads that are not blocking it. However, because signals need to be handled only once, a signal is typically delivered only to the first thread found that is not blocking it. The standard UNIX function for delivering a signal is kill (aid_t aid, int signal); here, we specify the process (aid) to which a particular signal is to be delivered. However,

POSIX Pthreads also provides the pthreadJkill(pthread_ttid, int signal) function, which allows a signal to be delivered to a specified thread (tid.) Although Windows does not explicitly provide support for signals, they can be emulated using asynchronous procedure calls (APCs). The APC facility allows a user thread to specify a function that is to be called when the user thread receives notification of a particular event. As indicated by its name, an APC is roughly equivalent to an asynchronous signal in UNIX. However, whereas UNIX must contend with how to deal with signals in a multithreaded environment, the APC facility is more straightforward, as an APC is delivered to a particular thread rather than a process.

Thread Pools

Whenever the server receives a request, it creates a separate thread to service the request. Whereas creating a separate thread is certainly superior to creating a separate process, a multithreaded server nonetheless has potential problems. The first concerns the amount of time required to create the thread prior to servicing the request, together with the fact that this thread will be discarded once it has completed its work. The second issue is more troublesome: If we allow all concurrent requests to be serviced in a new thread, we have not placed a bound on the number of threads concurrently active in the system. Unlimited threads could exhaust system resources, such as CPU time or memory. One solution to this issue is to use a thread pool. The general idea behind a thread pool is to create a number of threads at process startup and place them into a pool, where they sit and wait for work. When a server receives a request, it awakens a thread from this pool—if one is available-and passes it the request to service. Once the thread completes its service, it returns to the pool and awaits more work. If the pool contains no available thread, the server waits until one becomes free. Thread pools offer these benefits:

a. Servicing a request with an existing thread is usually faster than waiting to create a thread.

b. A thread pool limits the number of threads that exist at any one point. This is particularly important on systems that cannot support a large number of concurrent threads.

The number of threads in the pool can be set heuristically based on factors such as the number of CPUs in the system, the amount of physical memory, and the expected number of concurrent client requests. More sophisticated thread-pool architectures can dynamically adjust the number of threads in the pool according to usage patterns. Such architectures provide the further benefit of having a smaller pool—thereby consuming less memory—when the load on the system is low.

The Win32 API provides several functions related to thread pools. Using the thread pool API is similar to creating a thread with the Thread Create() function, as described in Section 4.3.2. Here, a function that is to run as a separate thread is defined. Such a function may appear as follows:

DWORD WINAPI PoolFunction(AVOID Param)
{ /** * this function runs as a separate thread. **/}

A pointer to PoolFunctionQ is passed to one of the functions in the thread pool API, and a thread from the pool executes this function.

One such member in the thread pool API is the QueueUserWorkltemO function, which is passed three parameters:

- LPTHREAD_START-ROUTINE Function: A pointer to the function that is to run as a separate thread
- PVOID Param: The parameter passed to Function
- ULONG Flags: Flags indicating how the thread pool is to create and manage execution of the thread

An example of an invocation is:

QueueUserWorkltemC&PoolFunction, NULL, 0);

This causes a thread from the thread pool to invoke PoolFunction () on behalf of the programmer. In this instance, we pass no parameters to PoolFunction (). Because we specify 0 as a flag, we provide the thread pool with no special instructions for thread creation. Other members in the Win32 thread pool API include utilities that invoke functions at periodic intervals or when an asynchronous I/O request completes. The java.util. concurrent package in Java 1.5 provides a thread pool utility as well.

Thread-Specific Data

Threads belonging to a process share the data of the process. Indeed, this sharing of data provides one of the benefits of multithreaded programming. However, in some circumstances, each thread might need its own copy of certain data. We will call such data thread-specific data. For example, in a transaction-processing system, we might service each transaction in a separate thread. Furthermore, each transaction may be assigned a unique identifier. To associate each thread with its unique identifier, we could use thread-specific data. Most thread libraries—including Win32 and Pthreads—provide some form of support for thread-specific data. Java provides support as well.

Scheduler Activations

A final issue to be considered with multithreaded programs concerns communication between the kernel and the thread library, which may be required by the many-to-many and two-level models. Such coordination allows the number of kernel threads to be dynamically adjusted to help ensure the best performance. Many systems implementing either the many-to-many or two-level model place an intermediate data structure between the user and kernel threads. This data structure-typically known as a lightweight process, or LWP-is shown in Figure 2.12. To the user-thread library, the LWP appears to be a virtual processor on which the application can schedule a user thread to run. Each LWP is attached to a kernel thread, and it is kernel threads that the operating system schedules to run on physical processors. If a kernel thread blocks (such as while waiting for an I/O operation to complete), the LWP blocks as well. Up the, chain, the user-level thread attached to the LWP also blocks.

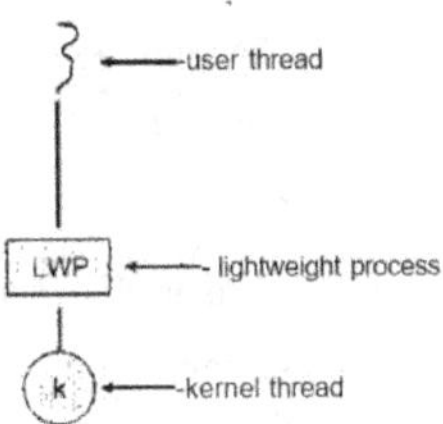

Figure 2.12: Lightweight Process (LWP)

An application may require any number of LWPs to run efficiently. Consider a CPU-bound application running on a single processor. In this scenario, only one thread can run at once, so one LWP is sufficient. An application that is I/O intensive may require multiple LWPs to execute, however. Typically, an LWP is required for each concurrent blocking system call. Suppose, for example, that five different file-read requests occur simultaneously. Five LWPs are needed, because all could be waiting for I/O completion in the kernel. If a process has only four LWPs, then the fifth request must wait for one of the LWPs to return from the kernel. One scheme for communication between the user-thread library and the kernel is known as scheduler activation. It works as follows: The kernel provides an application with a set of virtual processors (LWPs), and the application can schedule user threads onto an available virtual processor. Furthermore, the kernel must inform an application about certain events. This procedure is known as an upcall. Upcalls are handled by the thread library with an upcall handler, and upcall handlers must run on a virtual processor. One event that triggers an upcall occurs when an application thread is about to block. In this scenario, the kernel makes an upcall to the application informing it that a thread is about to block and identifying the specific thread. The kernel then allocates a new virtual processor to the application. The application runs an upcall handler on this new virtual processor, which saves the state of the blocking thread and relinquishes the virtual processor on which the blocking thread is running. The upcall handler then schedules another thread that is eligible to run on the new virtual processor. When the event that the blocking thread was waiting for occurs, the kernel makes another upcall to the thread library informing it that the previously blocked thread is now eligible to run. The upcall handler for this event also requires a virtual processor, and the kernel may allocate a new virtual processor or preempt one of the user threads and run the upcall handler on its virtual processor. After marking the unblocked thread as eligible to run, the application schedules an eligible thread to run on an available virtual processor.

2.13. Summary

To hide the effects of interrupts, operating systems provide a conceptual model consisting of sequential processes running in parallel. Processes can be created and terminated dynamically. Each process has its own address space.

For some applications it is useful to have multiple threads of control within a single process. These threads are scheduled independently and each one has its own stack, but all the threads in a process share a common address space. Threads can be implemented in user space or in the kernel.

Processes can communicate with one another using interprocess communication primitives, such as semaphores, monitors, or messages. These primitives are used to ensure that no two processes are ever in their critical regions at the same time, a situation that leads to chaos. A process can be running, runnable, or blocked and can change state when it or another process executes one of the interprocess communication primitives. Interthread communication is similar. Interprocess communication primitives can be used to solve such problems as the producer-consumer, dining philosophers, and reader-writer. Even with these primitives, care has to be taken to avoid errors and deadlocks.

A great many scheduling algorithms have been studied. Some of these are primarily used for batch systems, such as shortest job first scheduling. Others are common in both batch systems and interactive systems. These algorithms include round robin, priority scheduling, multilevel queues, guaranteed scheduling, lottery scheduling, and fair-share scheduling. Some systems make a clean separation between the scheduling mechanism and the scheduling policy, which allows users to have control of the scheduling algorithm.

CHAPTER 3

MEMORY MANAGEMENT

3.1. Introduction

Since main memory is usually too small to accommodate all the data and programs permanently, the computer system must provide secondary storage to back up main memory. Modern computer systems use disks as the primary on-line storage medium for information (both programs and data). The file system provides the mechanism for on-line storage of and access to both data and programs residing on the disks. A file is a collection of related information defined by its creator. The files are mapped by the operating system onto physical devices. Files are normally f organized into directories for ease of use.

The devices that attach to a computer vary in many aspects. Some devices transfer a character or a block of characters at a time. Some can be accessed only sequentially, others randomly. Some transfer data synchronously, others asynchronously. Some are dedicated, some shared. They can be read-only or read-write. They vary greatly in speed. In many ways, they are also the slowest major component of the computer.

Because of all this device variation, the operating system needs to provide a wide range of functionality to applications, to allow them to control all aspects of the devices. One key goal of an operating system's I/O subsystem is to provide the simplest interface possible to the rest of the system. Because devices are a performance bottleneck, another key is to optimize I/O for maximum concurrency.

The main purpose of a computer system is to execute programs. These programs, together with the data they access, must be in main memory (at least partially) during execution.

To improve both the utilization of the CPU and the speed of its response to users, the computer must keep several processes in memory. Many memory-management schemes exist, reflecting various approaches, and the effectiveness of each algorithm depends on the situation. Selection of a memory-management scheme for a system depends on many factors, especially on the hardware design of the system. Each algorithm requires its own hardware support.

- In a very simple OS, only one program at a time is in the memory. To run second program, the first one has to be removed and the second one placed in memory. Single Tasking System.

- More sophisticated OSs allows multiple programs to be in memory at the same time. To keep them from interfering with one another (and with OS), some kind of protection mechanism is needed. Multi-Tasking System.

- Main memory is a large array of words or bytes, ranging in size from hundreds of thousands to billions. Each word or byte has its own address.

- The central processor reads instructions from main memory during the instruction-fetch cycle and both reads and writes data from main memory during the data-fetch cycle (on Von Neumann architecture).

- For a program to be executed, it must be mapped to absolute addresses and loaded into memory. As the program executes, it accesses program instructions and data from memory by generating these absolute addresses. Eventually, the program terminates, its memory space is declared available, and the next program can be loaded and executed.

- The OS is responsible for the following activities in connection with memory management:
    - Keeping track of which parts of memory are currently being used and by whom,
    - Deciding which processes (or parts thereof) and data to move into and out of memory.
    - Allocating and de-allocating memory space as needed.

3.2.   Contiguous Allocation

Contiguous memory allocation is one of the efficient ways of allocating main memory to the processes. The memory is divided into two partitions. One for the Operating System and another for the user processes. Operating System is placed in low or high memory depending on the interrupt vector placed. In contiguous memory allocation each process is contained in a single contiguous section of memory.

Memory Protection

Memory protection is required to protect Operating System from the user processes and user processes from one another. A relocation register contains the value of the smallest physical address for example say 100040. The limit register contains the range of logical address for example say 74600. Each logical address must be less than limit register. If a logical address is greater than the limit register, then there is an addressing error and it is trapped. The limit register hence offers memory protection. The MMU, that is, Memory Management Unit maps the logical address dynamically, that is at run time, by adding the logical address to the value in relocation register. This added value is the physical memory address which is sent to the memory. The CPU scheduler selects a process for execution and a dispatcher loads the limit and relocation registers with correct values. The advantage of relocation register is that it provides an efficient way to allow the Operating System size to change dynamically.

Memory Allocation

There are two methods namely, multiple partition method and a general fixed partition method. In multiple partition method, the memory is divided into several fixed size partitions. One process occupies each partition. This scheme is rarely used nowadays. Degree of multiprogramming depends on the number of partitions.

Degree of multiprogramming is the number of programs that are in the main memory. The CPU is never left idle in multiprogramming. This was used by IBM OS/360 called MFT. MFT stands for Multiprogramming with a fixed number of Tasks.

Generalization of fixed partition scheme is used in MVT. MVT stands for Multiprogramming with a Variable number of Tasks. The Operating System keeps track of which parts of memory are available and which is occupied. This is done with the help of a table that is maintained by the Operating System. Initially the whole of the available memory is treated as one large block of memory called a hole. The programs that enter a system are maintained in an input queue. From the hole, blocks of main memory are allocated to the programs in the input queue. If the hole is large, then it is split into two, and one half is allocated to the arriving process and the other half is returned. As and when memory is allocated, a set of holes in scattered. If holes are adjacent, they can be merged.

Now there comes a general dynamic storage allocation problem. The following are the solutions to the dynamic storage allocation problem.

- First fit: The first hole that is large enough is allocated. Searching for the holes starts from the beginning of the set of holes or from where the previous first fit search ended.
- Best fit: The smallest hole that is big enough to accommodate the incoming process is allocated. If the available holes are ordered, then the searching can be reduced.
- Worst fit: The largest of the available holes is allocated.

First and best fits decrease time and storage utilization. First fit is generally faster.

3.3. Fragmentation

The disadvantage of contiguous memory allocation is fragmentation. There are two types of fragmentation, namely, internal fragmentation and External fragmentation.

Internal Fragmentation

When memory is free internally, that is inside a process but it cannot be used, we call that fragment as internal fragment. For example say a hole of size 18464 bytes is available. Let the size of the process be 18462. If the hole is allocated to this process, then two bytes are left which is not used. These two bytes which cannot be used forms the internal fragmentation. The worst part of it is that the overhead to maintain these two bytes is more than two bytes.

External Fragmentation

All the three dynamic storage allocation methods discussed above suffer external fragmentation. When the total memory space that is got by adding the scattered holes is sufficient to satisfy a request but it is not available contiguously, then this type of fragmentation is called external fragmentation.

The solution to this kind of external fragmentation is compaction. Compaction is a method by which all free memory that are scattered are placed together in one large memory block. It is to be noted that compaction cannot be done if relocation is done at compile time or assembly time. It is possible only if dynamic relocation is done, that is relocation at execution time.

One more solution to external fragmentation is to have the logical address space and physical address space to be noncontiguous. Paging and Segmentation are popular non-contiguous allocation methods.

3.4. Partitioning

In a partitioning operating system, memory (and possibly CPU time as well) is divided among statically allocated partitions in a fixed manner. The idea is to take a processor and make it pretend it is several processors by completely isolating the subsystems.

Hard partitions are set up for each part of the system and each has certain amount of memory (and potentially a time slice) allocated to it. Each partition is forever limited to its initial fixed memory allocation, which can neither be increased nor decreased after the initial system configuration.

Within each partition may be multiple threads or processes, or both, if the operating system supports them. How these threads are scheduled depends on the implementation of the OS. A partition will generally support a separate namespace to enable multi-programming by mapping the program into the partition. If the operating system supports time partitioning, it too is fixed. For example, in an ARINC 653 partitioning system with just three partitions and a total major allocation of 100ms per cycle, a fixed cyclic scheduler could be set to run the first partition for 20 ms, then the second partition for 30 ms, and then the third for 50 ms.

3.5. Paging

When a program is selected for execution, the system brings it into virtual storage, divides it into pages of four kilobytes, and transfers the pages into central storage for execution. To the programmer, the entire program appears to occupy contiguous space in storage at all times. Actually, not all pages of a program are necessarily in central storage, and the pages that are in central storage do not necessarily occupy contiguous space.

The pieces of a program executing in virtual storage must be moved between real and auxiliary storage. To allow this, z/OS® manages storage in units, or blocks, of four kilobytes. The following blocks are defined:

- A block of central storage is a frame.
- A block of virtual storage is a page.
- A block of auxiliary storage is a slot.

Most modern computers have special hardware called a memory management unit (MMU). This unit sits between the CPU and the memory unit. Whenever the CPU wants to access memory (whether it is to load an instruction or load or store data), it sends the desired memory address to the MMU, which translates it to another address before passing it on the memory unit. The address generated by the CPU, after any indexing or other addressing-mode arithmetic, is called a virtual address, and the address it gets translated to by the MMU is called a physical address.

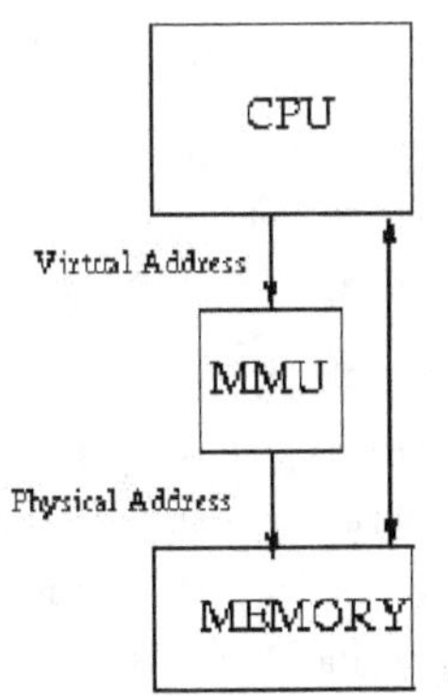

Figure 3.1: Memory Management Unit

Normally, the translation is done at the granularity of a page. Each page is a power of 2 bytes long, usually between 1024 and 8192 bytes. If virtual address p is mapped to physical address f (where p is a multiple of the page size), then address p+o is mapped to physical address f+o for any offset o less than the page size. In other words, each page is mapped to a contiguous region of physical memory called a page frame.

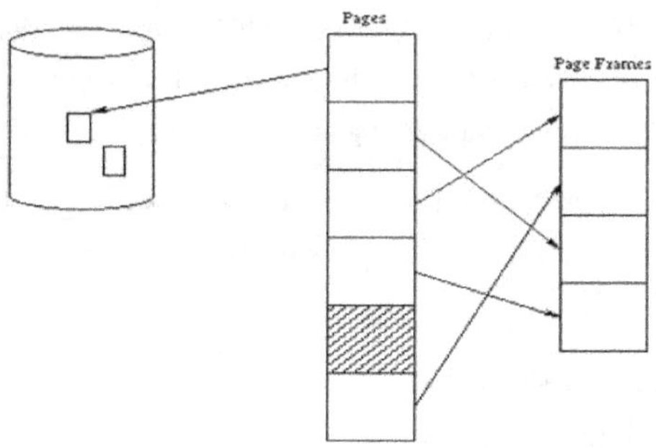

Figure 3.2: Page Frames

The MMU allows a contiguous region of virtual memory to be mapped to page frames scattered around physical memory making life much easier for the OS when allocating memory. Much more importantly, however, it allows infrequently-used pages to be stored on disk. Here's how it works: The tables used by the MMU have a valid bit for each page in the virtual address space. If this bit is set, the translation of virtual addresses on a page proceeds as normal. If it is clear, any attempt by the CPU to access an address on the page generates an interrupt called a page fault trap. The OS has an interrupt handler for page faults, just as it has a handler for any other kind of interrupt. It is the job of this handler to get the requested page into memory.

In somewhat more detail, when a page fault is generated for page p1, the interrupt handler does the following:

- Find out where the contents of page p1 are stored on disk. The OS keeps this information in a table. It is possible that this page isn't anywhere at all, in which case the memory reference is simply a bug. In this case, the OS takes some corrective action such as killing the process that made the reference (this is source of the notorious message —"memory fault -- core dumped"). Assuming the page is on disk:

- Find another page p2 mapped to some frame f of physical memory that is not used much.

- Copy the contents of frame f out to disk.

- Clear page p2's valid bit so that any subsequent references to page p2 will cause a page fault.

- Copy page p1's data from disk to frame f.

- Update the MMU's tables so that page p1 is mapped to frame f.

- Return from the interrupt, allowing the CPU to retry the instruction that caused the interrupt.

3.6.   Segmentation

Memory segmentation is the division of computer's primary memory into segments or sections. In a computer system using segmentation, a reference to a memory location includes a value that identifies a segment and an offset within that segment. Segments or sections are also used in object files of compiled programs when they are linked together into a program image and when the image is loaded into memory.

Different segments may be created for different program modules, or for different classes of memory usage such as code and data segments. Certain segments may even be shared between programs

- An important aspect of memory management that became unavoidable with paging is the separation of the user's view of memory and the actual physical memory.

- The user's view of memory is not the same as the actual physical memory. The user's view is mapped onto physical memory.

- This mapping allows differentiation between logical memory and physical memory.

Segmentation and Paging

Use two levels of mapping, with logical sizes for objects, to make tables manageable.

- Each segment contains one or more pages.

- Segment corresponds to logical units: code, data, and stack. Segments vary in size and are often large. Pages are for the use of the OS; they are fixed size to make it easy to manage memory.

- Going from paging to P+S is like going from single segment to multiple segments, except at a higher level. Instead of having a single page table, have many page tables with a base and bound for each. Call the stuff associated with each page table a segment.

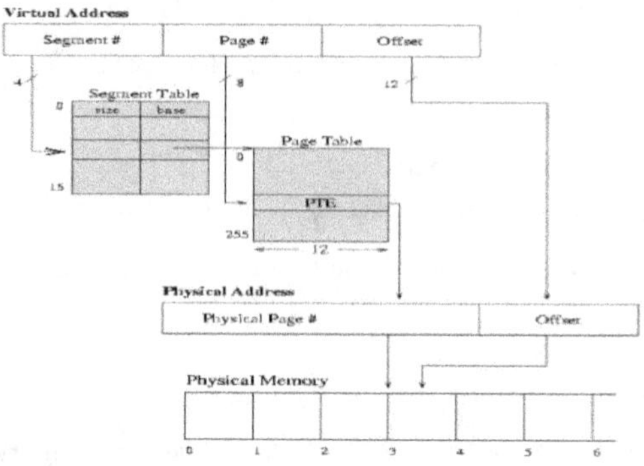

Figure 3.3: Levels of Mapping

System 370 example: 24-bit virtual address space, 4 bits of segment number, 8 bits of page number, and 12 bits of offset. Segment table contains real address of page table along with the length of the page table (a sort of bounds register for the segment). Page table entries are only 12 bits, real addresses are 24 bits.

- If a segment is not used, then there is no need to even have a page table for it.
- Can share at two levels: single page, or single segment (whole page table).

Pages eliminate external fragmentation, and make it possible for segments to grow without any reshuffling.

If page size is small compared to most segments, then internal fragmentation is not too bad.

The user is not given access to the paging tables.

If translation tables are kept in main memory, overheads could be very high: 1 or 2 overhead references for every real reference.

Another example: VAX.

- Address is 32 bits, top two select segments. Three base-bound pairs define page tables (system, P0, P1).
- Pages are 512 bytes long.
- Read-write protection information is contained in the page table entries, not in the segment table.
- One segment contains operating system stuff; two contain stuff of current user process.
- Potential problem: page tables can get big. Do not want to have to allocate them contiguously, especially for large user processes.

Solution:

- System base-bounds pairs are physical addresses, system tables must be contiguous.
- User base-bounds pairs are virtual addresses in the system space. This allows the user page tables to be scattered in non-contiguous pages of physical memory.
- The result is a two-level scheme.

In current systems, you will see three and even four-level schemes to handle 64-bit address spaces.

Demand Paging

As there is much less physical memory than virtual memory the operating system must be careful that it does not use the physical memory inefficiently. One way to save physical memory is to only load virtual pages that are currently being used by the executing program. For example, a database program may be run to query a database. In this case not all of the database needs to be loaded into memory, just those data records that are being examined. Also, if the database query is a search query then the it does not make sense to load the code from the database program that deals with adding new records. This technique of only loading virtual pages into memory as they are accessed is known as demand paging.

When a process attempts to access a virtual address that is not currently in memory the CPU cannot find a page table entry for the virtual page referenced. For example, in Figure there is no entry in Process X's page table for virtual PFN 2 and so if Process X attempts to read from an address within virtual PFN 2 the CPU cannot translate the address into a physical one. At this point the CPU cannot cope and needs the operating system to fix things up. It notifies the operating system that a page fault has occurred and the operating system makes the process wait whilst it fixes things up. The CPU must bring the appropriate page into memory from the image on disk. Disk access takes a long time, relatively speaking, and so the process must wait quite a while until the page has been fetched. If there are other processes that could run then the operating system will select one of them to run. The fetched page is written into a free physical page frame and an entry for the virtual PFN is added to the processes page table. The process is then restarted at the point where the memory fault occurred. This time the virtual memory access is made, the CPU can make the address translation and so the process continues to run. This is known as demand paging and occurs when the system is busy but also when an image is first loaded into memory. This mechanism means that a process can execute an image that only partially resides in physical memory at any one time.

3.7.   Research on Memory Management

Memory management, especially paging algorithms, was once a fruitful area for research, but most of that seems to have largely died off, at least for general purpose systems. Most real systems tend to use some variation on clock, because it is easy to implement and relatively effective. One recent exception, however, is a redesign of the 4.4 BSD virtual memory system (Cranor and Parulkar, 1999).

There is still research going on concerning paging in newer kinds of systems though. For example, cell phones and PDAs have become small PCs, and many of them page RAM to "disk," only disk on a cell phone is flash memory, which has different properties than a rotating magnetic disk. Some recent work is reported by (In et al., 2007; Joo et al., 2006; and Park et al., 2004a). Park et al. (2004b) have also looked at energy-aware demand paging in mobile devices.

Research is also taking place on modeling paging performance (Albers et al., 2002; Burton and Kelly, 2003; Cascaval et al., 2005; Panagiotou and Souza, 2006; and Peserico, 2003). Also of interest is memory management for multimedia systems (Dasigenis et al., 2001; Hand, 1999) and real-time systems (Pizlo and Vitek, 2006).

3.8.   Summary

In this chapter we have examined memory management. We saw that the simplest systems do not swap or page at all. Once a program is loaded into memory, it remains there in place until it finishes. Some operating systems allow only one process at a time in memory, while others support multiprogramming.

The next step up is swapping. When swapping is used, the system can handle more processes than it has room for in memory. Processes for which there is no room are swapped out to the disk. Free space in memory and on disk can be kept track of with a bitmap or a hole list.

Modern computers often have some form of virtual memory. In the simplest form, each process' address space is divided up into uniform-sized blocks called pages, which can be placed into any available page frame in memory. There are many page replacement algorithms; two of the better algorithms are aging and WSClock.

Paging systems can be modeled by abstracting the page reference string from the program and using the same reference string with different algorithms. These models can be used to make some predictions about paging behavior.

To make paging systems work well, choosing an algorithm is not enough; attention to such issues as determining the working set, memory allocation policy, and page size is required.

Segmentation helps in handling data structures that change size during execution and simplifies linking and sharing. It also facilitates providing different protection for different segments. Sometimes segmentation and paging are combined to provide a two-dimensional virtual memory. The MULTICS system and the Intel Pentium support segmentation and paging.

CHAPTER 4

DEADLOCK

Computer systems are full of resources that can only be used by one process at a time. Common examples include printers, tape drives, and slots in the system's internal tables. Having two processes simultaneously writing to the printer leads to gibberish. Having two processes using the same file system table slot invariably will lead to a corrupted file system. Consequently, all operating systems have the ability to (temporarily) grant a process exclusive access to certain resources.

For many applications, a process needs exclusive access to not one resource, but several. Suppose, for example, two processes each want to record a scanned document on a CD. Process A requests permission to use the scanner and is granted it. Process B is programmed differently and requests these CD recorder first and is also granted it. Now A asks for the CD recorder, but the request is denied until B releases it. Unfortunately, instead of releasing the CD recorder B asks for the scanner. At this point both processes are blocked and will remain so forever. This situation is called a deadlock.

Deadlocks can also occur across machines. For example, many offices have a local area network with many computers connected to it. Often devices such as scanners, CD recorders, printers, and tape drives are connected to the network as shared resources, available to any user on any machine. If these devices can be reserved remotely (i.e., from the user's home machine), the same kind of deadlocks can occur as described above. More complicated situations can cause deadlocks involving three, four, or more devices and users.

Deadlocks can occur in a variety of different situations besides requesting dedicated I/O devices. In a database system, for example, a program may have to lock several records it is using, to avoid race conditions. If process A locks record Rl and process B locks record R2, and then each process tries to lock the other one's record, we also have a deadlock. Thus deadlocks can occur on hardware resources or on software resources.

In this chapter, we will look at several kinds of deadlocks, see how they arise, and study some ways of preventing or avoiding them. Although this material is about deadlocks in the context of operating systems, they also occur in database systems and many other contexts in computer science, so this material is actually applicable to a wide variety of multiprocess systems. A great deal has been written about deadlocks. Two bibliographies on the subject have appeared in Operating Systems Review and should be consulted for references (Newton,

1979; and Zobel, 1983). Although these bibliographies are old, most of the work on deadlocks was done well before 1980, so they are still useful.

4.1.   Condition for Deadlock

In deadlock, processes never finish executing and system resources are tied up preventing other pending Jobs from starting.

Necessary condition: a dead lock situation can arise, in a system when the following four conditions hold simultaneously in a system.

1)   Mutual exclusion condition

2)   Hold and wait condition

3)   No pre-emption condition

4)   Circular wait condition

All four of these conditions must be present for a deadlock to occur. If one of them is absent, no deadlock is possible.

Mutual Exclusion Condition

Each resource is either currently assigned to exactly one process or is available.

Hold and Wait Condition

Processes currently holding resources granted earlier can request new resources.

No Preemption Condition

Resources cannot be pre-empted; that is, resources can be released only voluntarily by the process holding it, after that process has completed its task.

Circular Wait Condition

There must be a circular chain of the or more processes, each of which is waiting for a resource held by the next member of chain.

4.2.   Resources

A major class of deadlocks involve resources, so we will begin our study by seeing what they are. Deadlocks can occur when processes have been granted exclusive access to devices, data records, files, and so forth. To make the discussion of deadlocks as general as possible, we will refer to the objects granted as resources. A resource can be a hardware device (e.g., a tape drive) or a piece of information (e.g., a locked record in a database). A computer will normally have many different resources that can be acquired. For some resources, several identical instances may be available, such as three tape drives. When several copies of a resource are available, any one of them can be used to satisfy any request for the resource. In short, a resource is anything that must be acquired, used, and released over the course of time.

Preemptable and Nonpreemptable Resources

Resources come in two types: preemptable and nonpreemptable. A preemptable resource is one that can be taken away from the process owning it with no ill effects. Memory is an example of a preemptable resource. Consider, for example, a system with 256 MB of user memory, one printer, and two 256-MB processes that each want to print something. Process A requests and gets the printer, then starts to compute the values to print. Before it has finishc! With the computation, it exceeds its time quantum and is swapped out.

Process B now runs and tries, unsuccessfully, to acquire the prii j-v >tenially, we now have a deadlock situation; because A has the printer anu has the memory, and neither one can proceed without the resource held by the other.

Fortunately, it is possible to preempt (take away) the memory from B by swapping it out and swapping A in. Now A can run, do its printing, and then release the printer. No deadlock occurs.

A nonpreemptable resource, in contrast, is one that cannot be taken away from its current owner without causing the computation to fail. If a process has begun to bum a CD-ROM, suddenly taking the CD recorder away from it and giving it to another process will result in a garbled CD. CD recorders are not preemptable at an arbitrary moment.

In general, deadlocks involve nonpreemptable resources. Potential deadlocks that involve preemptable resources can usually be resolved by reallocating resources from one process to another. Thus our treatment will focus on nonpreemptable resources.

The sequence of events required to use a resource is given below in an abstract form.

- Request the resource.
- Use the resource.
- Release the resource.

If the resource is not available when it is requested, the requesting process is forced to wait. In some operating systems, the process is automatically blocked when a resource request fails, and awakened when it becomes available. In other systems, the request fails with an error code, and it is up to the calling process to wait a little while and try again. A process whose resource request has just been denied will normally sit in a tight loop requesting the resource, then sleeping, then trying again. Although this process is not blocked, for all intents and purposes it is as good as blocked, because it cannot do any useful work. In our further treatment, we will assume that when a process is denied a resource request, it is put to sleep.

The exact nature of requesting a resource is highly system dependent. In some systems, a request system call is provided to allow processes to explicitly ask for resources. In others, the only resources that the operating system knows about are special files that only one process can have open at a time. These are opened by the usual open call. If the file is already in use, the caller is blocked until its current owner closes it.

4.3.   Dead Lock Modelling

Hold (1972) showed how these four condition can be modelled using directed graph. The graphs have two kinds of nodes: process, shown as circles, and resources, shown as squares. An arc from a resource node(square) to a process node(circle) means that the resource has previously been requested by, granted to, and is currently held by that process.

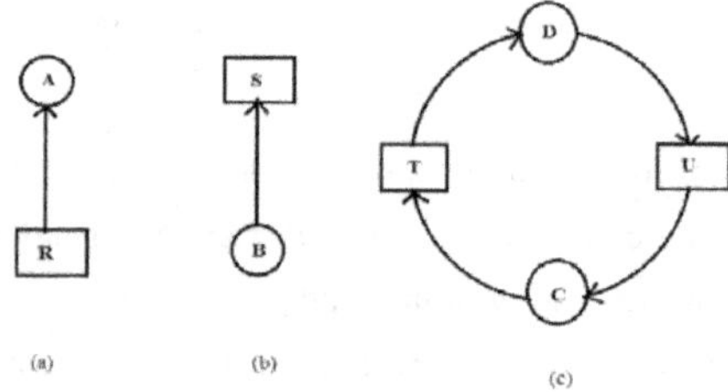

Figure 4.1: Resource Allocation Graph

In fig 4.1 (a) resource R is currently assigned to process to a resource means that the process is currently blocked waiting for that the process is currently blocked waiting for that resource. Fig(b) process B is waiting for resource S. Fig(c) we see a deadlock. Process C is waiting for resource T, which is currently held by process D. Process D is not about to release resource T because it is waiting for resource U, held by C. Both process will wait forever.

Now let us look at an example of how resource allocation graph can be used. Dead locks can be described in terms of a direct graph called a System Resource-allocation graph. The graph consist of a set of vertices V and a set edges E. V is partitioned into 2 types

P= {P0, P1 ...P_n} the set of all the processes in the system. And R= {R_0, R_1,........R_m} the set consist of all resource types in the system.

The directed edge from process Pi to resource type Rj is denoted by Pi→Rj, it signifies that process Pi requested an instance of resource type Rj and is currently waiting for that resource.

A directed edge from Resource type R_j to process P_i, is denoted $R_j→ P_i$ it signifies that an instance of resource type R_j has been allocated to process P_j. A direct edge $P_i →R_j$ is called an request edge; a directed edge $R_j →P_i$ is called an assignment edge.

A requests edge point to only the square Rj, where as an assignment edge must also designate one of the dots in the square. When a process Pi, requests an instance of resource type Rj, a request edge is inserted in the resource allocation graph. When this request can be fulfilled the request is instantaneously transformed to an assignment edge. Then the process later releases the resource. The resource-allocation graph below depicts the following situation.

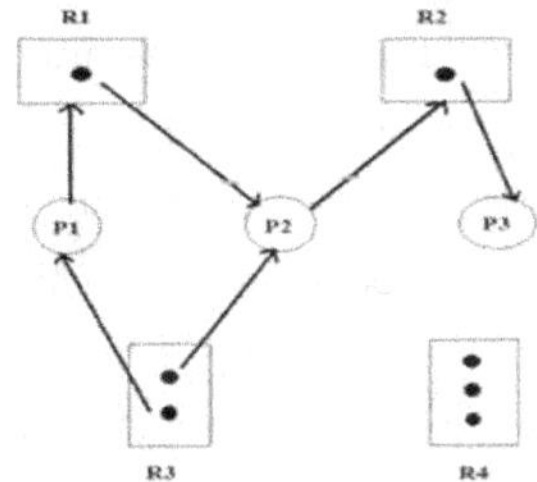

(i)   The sets P,R and E:

P= { $P_0, P_1, P_2, ...P_n$ }

R= { $R_0, R_1, ...R_m$ }

E= { $P_1 → R_1,\ P_2 → R_3,\ R_1 → P_2, R_2 → P_2, R_2 → P_1, R_3 → P_1$ }

(ii) Resources Instances

- One instance of resource type R_1.
- Two instance of resource type R_2.
- One instance of resource type R_3.
- Three instances of resource type R_4.

(iii) Process states

- Process P_1 is holding an instance of resource type R_2, and is waiting for an instance of resource type R_1.
- Process P_2 is holding an instance of R_1 and R_2, and is waiting for an instance of resource type R_3.
- Process P_3 is holding an instance of R_3.

4.4.   Deadlock Detection and Recovery

A second technique is detection and recovery. When this technique is used, the system does not attempt to prevent deadlocks from occurring. Instead, it lets them occur, tries to detect when this happens, and then takes some action to recover after the fact. In this section we will look at some of the ways deadlocks can be detected and some of the ways recovery from them can be handled. In a system where deadlock–prevention or avoidance algorithm are not used, then the system must provide:

1) An algorithm that examines the state of the system to determine whether a deadlock occurred.

2) An algorithm to recover from the deadlock.

Deadlock Detection with One Resource of Each Type

If all the resources in a system have only a single instance, then the deadlock detection algorithm can be defined using a variant of the resource allocation graph, called "wait for graph". This graph is obtained from the resource allocation graph by retaining the nodes of resource type and collapsing the proper edges that is an edge from Pi to Pj–in a wait for graph implies that process Pi is waiting for process Pj to release a resource that Pi needs. An edge Pi →Pj exists in a wait for graph, if and only if the corresponding Resource allocation graph contains 2 edges Pi →Rq and Rq →Pi for some resources Rq. Similar to our discussion, a Direct link exists in the system if and only if wait for Graph contains a cycle. Thus to detect a Direct link the system needs a maintain wait for graph and invoke the algorithm periodically which searches for a cycle in the graph.

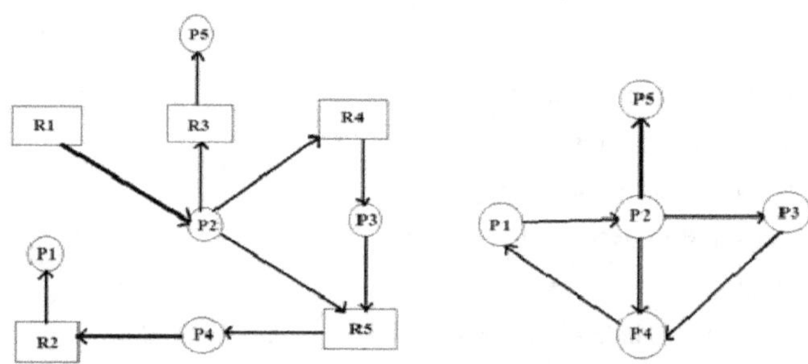

Figure 4.2: Resource Allocation Graph for Dead Lock

An algorithm requires an order of N2 operations to detect a cycle in a graph, where 'n' is the number of vertices in the graph.

Deadlock Detection with Multiple Resources of Each Type

The above wait for graph is not applicable to resources with multiple instances.

This algorithm employs some time varying data structure and is similar to those defined in Banker's Algorithm.

1) Available: A vector of length m indicates the number of resources available in each type.
2) Allocation: An n x m matrix defines the number of resources of each type currently allocated to each process.
3) Request: an n x m matrix indicates the current request of each process. If request [I,j] = k then process P_i is requesting K more instances of resource type R_j.

The detection algorithm checks every possible allocation sequences for the process that is to be completed.

1) Let's work and finish the vectors of length m and n, respectively. Initialize work : = Available. For i=1, 2, ..., n, if allocation i=0, then finish[i] : ≠ false; otherwise, finish[j] : + true.
2) Find an index I such that both
    * Finish [i] = false
    * Request :≤work

    if no such i exists, go to step 4.
3) Work := work + allocation i

    Finish[i] : = true

    Goto step 2.
4) Finish[i] = false, for some I, 1 ≤ i ≤ n, then the system is in deadlock state.

    Moreover if finish[i]= false, then process P_i is deadlocked.

This algorithm requires an order of m x n2 operations to detect whether the system is in a deadlocked state.

Recovery from Deadlock

Suppose that our deadlock detection algorithm has succeeded and detected a deadlock. What next? Some way is needed to recover and get the system going again.

In this section we will discuss various ways of recovering from deadlock. None of them are especially attractive, however.

Recovery through Preemption

In some cases it may be possible to temporarily take a resource away from its current owner and give it to another process. In many cases, manual intervention may be required, especially in batch processing operating systems running on mainframes.

For example, to take a laser printer away from its owner, the operator can collect all the sheets already printed and put them in a pile. Then the process can be suspended (marked as not runnable). At this point the printer can be assigned to another process. When that process finishes, the pile of printed sheets can be put back in the printer's output tray and the original process restarted.

The ability to take a resource away from a process, have another process use it, and then give it back without the process noticing it is highly dependent on the nature of the resource. Recovering this way is frequently difficult or impossible. Choosing the process to suspend depends largely on which ones have resources that can easily be taken back.

Recovery through Rollback

If the system designers and machine operators know that deadlocks are likely, they can arrange to have processes check pointed periodically. Check pointing a process means that its state is written to a file so that it can be restarted later. The checkpoint contains not only the memory image, but also the resource state, in other words, which resources are currently assigned to the process. To be most effective, new checkpoints should not overwrite old ones but should be written to new fades, so as the process executes, a whole sequence accumulates.

When a deadlock is detected, it is easy to see which resources are needed. To do the recovery, a process that owns a needed resource is rolled back to a point in time before it acquired that resource by starting one of its earlier checkpoints. All the work done since the checkpoint is lost (e.g., output printed since the checkpoint must be discarded, since it will be printed again).

In effect, the process is reset to an earlier moment when it did not have the resource, which is now assigned to one of the deadlocked processes. If the restarted process tries to acquire the resource again, it will have to wait until it becomes available.

Recovery through Killing Processes

The crudest, but simplest way to break a deadlock is to kill one or more processes. One possibility is to kill a process in the cycle. With a little luck, the other processes will be able to continue. If this does not help, it can be repeated until the cycle is broken.

Alternatively, a process not in the cycle can be chosen as the victim in order to release its resources. In this approach, the process to be killed is carefully chosen because it is holding resources that some process in the cycle needs. For example, one process might hold a printer and want a plotter, with another process holding a plotter and wanting a printer. These two are deadlocked. A third process may hold another identical printer and another identical plotter and be happily running. Killing the third process will release these resources and break the deadlock involving the first two.

Where possible, it is best to kill a process that can be rerun from the beginning with no ill effects. For example, a compilation can always be rerun because all it does is read a source file and produce an object file. If it is killed partway through, the first run has no influence on the second run.

On the other hand, a process that updates a database cannot always be run a second time safely. If the process adds 1 to some field of a table in the database, running it once, killing it, and then running it again will add 2 to the field, which is incorrect.

4.5.   Deadlock Avoidance

Prevention of deadlocks using previous methods results in low device utilization and reduced system inputs. For avoiding deadlocks, requires additional information about how resources are to be requested. Various Algorithms differ in Amount and type of information requires. One model requires that each process declare the maximum number of resources of each type that it may need. A deadlock avoidance approach, dynamically examines the resource allocation state to ensure that there can never be a circular wait condition. The resource allocation state is defined by the number of available and allocated resources and maximum demands of the processes.

Safe State and Unsafe State

A state is safe if the System is able to allocate resources to each Process. In some order and avoid a deadlock. More formally, a system is in a Safe state only if there exists a safe sequence.

A sequence of Process < P1, P2, ...Pn> is a safe Sequence for the current allocation state if for each Pi, the resources that Pi can still request can be satisfied by the currently available resources plus the resources held by all the Pi with j <i.

In this situation, if the resources that process Pi needs are not immediately available, the Pi needs are not immediately available, the Pi can wait until all of its needed resources, complete its desired took, and return its allocated resources and terminates.

When Pi terminates, Pi can obtain its needed resources and so on. If no such sequence exists, then the system state is said to be unsafe.

A safe state is not a deadlock state. Not all unsafe state are called deadlocks, however, an unsafe state may lead to a deadlock.

As long as the state is safe, the operating system can avoid unsafe states. In an unsafe state, the operating system cannot prevent process from requesting resources such that a deadlock occurs. Behaviour of the process controls unsafe states.

Example: consider a system with 12 magnetic Tape drives and a 3 process: P0, P1, and P2

Process P0 requires – 10 tape drives

Process P_1 requires – 04 tape drives

Process P_2 requires – 09 tape drives

Suppose at time, t_0, P_0 is holding 5 tape drives P_1 is holding 2 and P_2 is holding 2 tape drives.

Maximum needs	Current needs	Available
P_0 10	5	(5 rem + 5 all = 10) =10 rem
P_1 04	2	(3 rem + 2 released = 5) = 5 rem
P_2 09	2	(= 12 – 9 = 03 total)

So at to-system is in safe state sequence <P0, P1, P2> satisfies safety condition. Since, P1 can immediately be allocated all its tape drives and then returns them out of 9 currently allocated, the process P1 can get all its tape drives and return them and finally P2 could get all its tape drives and return them. It is possible to go from a sage state to an unsafe state. Suppose at t1, P2 requests and it is allocated 1 more tape drive, then the system is no longer in a safe state. At this point, only P2 can be allocated all its tape drives. When it returns then the system will have only 4 available tape drives since P0 is allocated 5 tape drives, but has a maximum of 10, it may request 5 more, since they are unavailable, process P0 must wait. Similarly P2 may request an additional 6 tape drives and will have to wait, resulting in a deadlock. A given safe state avoidance algorithm can be defined to ensure the system will never deadlock.

<pre>
                              At $t_1 P_2 = 10$

         Maximum needs   current needs

    P_0 10   5   (4 rem + 5 allocated = 9) - wait
    P_1 04   2   (2 rem + 2 allocated = 4) = 4 rem
    P_2 09   2+1   2 + 1 (additional request)
                                                   10 = 12 – 10 = 2 rem
</pre>

P_2 = 3 resource allocated → needs to more to reach maximum, so P_2 also waits.

Banker's Algorithm

A resource allocation graph is not applicable to a resource allocation system with multiple instances of each resource type. The algorithm, which can be used to avoid deadlock in such system, which is less efficient than Resource Allocation Graph algorithm, is Bankers Algorithm. When a new process enters the system, it must declare the maximum number of instances of each resources type that it may need and this number may not exceed the total number of resources in the system.

When there is a request, the system must determine whether allocation of the resources leaves the system in a safe state. If yes, resources are allocated, otherwise the process must wait until some other process releases enough resources. Several data structures must be defined to implement Bankers Algorithm. These data structures encode the state of the resource–allocation systems. Let 'n' be the number of Processes in the system and 'm' be the number of resources types.

Data structures required are
1) Available
2) Max
3) Allocation
4) Need

Available

A vector of length m indicates the number of available resources of each type. If Available[j] = k, these are k instances of resource type R_j available.

Max

An n x m matrix defines the maximum demand of each process. If Max[i, j] = k, then P_i may request at most k instances of resource type R_j.

Allocation

A n x m matrix defines the number of resources of each type currently allocated to each process. If Allocation [i, j] = k, then process P_i currently allocated k instances of resource type R_j.

Need

An n x m matrix indicates the remaining resource need of each process. If need[i, j] = k, then P_i may need k more instances of resource type R_j to complete its task. Note that Need[i,j] = Max[i,j] – Allocation[i, j].

1) *Safety Algorithm*

In order to find whether a system is in a safe state, the algorithm can be defined as:

1) Let work and finish be vectors of length m and n, respectively. Initialize work := Available. For i=1,2,,,,,,n, if allocation:$\neq$0 then finish[i]:= false; otherwise, finish[i] := true.

2) Find an i such that both

   - Finish[i] = false
   - $Request_i \leq work$.

     If no such I exists, go a step 4.

3) Work : = work + $Allocation_i$

   - Finish[i] : = true
   - Goto step 2.

4) Finish[i] = true for all I, then the system is in a safe state.

This algorithm may require an order of m x n^2 operations to decide whether the system is in a safe state.

2) *Resource–Request Algorithm*

Let request I, be the request vector for process P_i. If $request_i[j]$ = k, then P_i wants k instances of type R_j. When a request for resource is made by P_i, the following actions are taken.

1) If $request_i \leq need_i$, go to step 2. Otherwise, raise all error condition, since the process has exceeded its maximum claim.

2) If Request < available, go to step 3. Otherwise , P_i must wait, since the resources are not available.

3) Have the system pretenmd to have allocated the requested resources to process P_i by modifying the state as follows:

   Available := Available – $Request_i$;

   $Allocation_i$:= allocation + $request_i$;

   $Need_i$:= Need _ $Request_i$;

If the resulting resource–allocation state is safe, then the transaction is completed and Process P_i is allocated its resources.

If new state is unsafe, then P_i must wait for request i and the old resource–allocation state is restored.

4.6. Deadlock Prevention

Having seen that deadlock avoidance is essentially impossible, because it requires information about future requests, which is not known, how do real systems avoid deadlock? The answer is to go back to the four conditions stated by Coffman et al. (1971) to see if they can provide a clue. If we can ensure that at least one of these conditions is never satisfied, then deadlocks will be structurally impossible (Havender, 1968).

Attacking the Mutual Exclusion Condition

First let us attack the mutual exclusion condition. If no resource were ever assigned exclusively to a single process, we would never have deadlocks. However, it is equally clear that allowing two processes to write on the printer at the same time will lead to chaos. By spooling printer output, several processes can generate output at the same time. In this model, the only process that actually requests the physical printer is the printer daemon. Since the daemon never requests any other resources, we can eliminate deadlock for the printer.

If the daemon is programmed to begin printing even before all the output is spooled, the printer might lie idle if an output process decides to wait several hours after the first burst of output. For this reason, daemons are normally programmed to print only after the complete output file is available.

However, this decision itself could lead to deadlock. What would happen if two processes each filled up one half of the available spooling space with output and neither was finished producing its full output? In this case we have two processes that kve each finished part, but not all, of their output, and cannot continue. Neither process will ever finish, so we have a deadlock on the disk. Nevertheless, there is a germ of an idea here that is frequently applicable. Avoid assigning a resource when that is not absolutely necessary, and try to make sure that as few processes as possible may actually claim the resource.

Attacking the Hold and Wait Condition

The second of the conditions stated by Coffman et al. looks slightly more promising. If we can prevent processes that hold resources from waiting for more resources, we can eliminate deadlocks. One way to achieve this goal is to require all processes to request all their resources before starting execution. If everything is available, the process will be allocated whatever it needs and can run to completion. If one or more resources are busy, nothing will be allocated and the process would just wait An immediate problem with this approach is that many processes do not know how many resources they will need until they have started running.

In fact, if they knew, the banker's algorithm could be used. Another problem is that resources will not be used optimally with this approach. Take, as an example, a process that reads data from an input tape, analyzes it for an hour, and then writes , an output tape as well as plotting the results.

If all resources must be requested in advance, the process will tie up the output tape drive and the plotter for an hour. Nevertheless, some mainframe batch systems require the user to list all the resources on the first line of each job.

The system then acquires all resources immediately and keeps them until the job finishes. While this method puts a burden on the programmer and wastes resources, it does prevent deadlocks. A slightly different way to break the hold-and-wait condition is to require a process requesting a resource to first temporarily release all the resources it currently holds. Then it tries to get everything it needs all at once.

Attacking the No Preemption Condition

Attacking the third condition (no preemption) is also a possibility If a process has been assigned the printer and is in the middle of printing its output, forcibly taking away the printer because a needed plotter is not available is tricky at best and impossible at worst. However, some resources can be virtualized to avoid this situation. Spooling printer output to the disk and allowing only the printer daemon access to the real printer eliminates deadlocks involving the printer, although it creates one for disk space. With large disks, however, running out of disk space is unlikely. However, not all resources can be virtualized like this. For example, records in databases or tables inside the operating system.

Attacking the Circular Wait Condition

Only one condition is left. The circular wait can be eliminated in several ways. One way is simply to have a rule saying that a process is entitled only to a single resource at any moment. If it needs a second one, it must release the first one. For a process that needs to copy a huge file from a tape to a printer, this restriction is unacceptable.

Another way to avoid the circular wait is to provide a global numbering of all the resources, as shown in Fig. 4.3(a).

Now the rule is this: processes can request resources whenever they want to, but all requests must be made in numerical order. A process may request first a printer and then a tape drive, but it may not request first a plotter and then a printer.

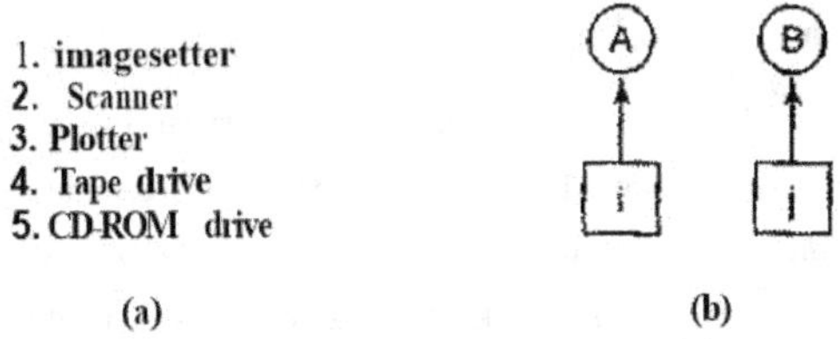

Figure 4.3: (a) Numerically Ordered Resources, (b) A Resource Graph

With this rule, the resource allocation graph can never have cycles. Let us see why this is true for the case of two processes, in Fig. 4.3(b). We can get a deadlock only if A requests resource j and B requests resource i. Assuming i and j are distinct resources, they will have different numbers. If i > j, then A is not allowed to request j because that is lower than what it already has. If i < j, then B is not allowed to request i because that is lower than what it already has. Either way, deadlock is impossible.

With more than two processes, the same logic holds. At every instant, one of the assigned resources will be highest. The process holding that resource will never ask for a resource already assigned. It will either finish, or at worst, request even higher numbered resources, all of which are available. Eventually, it will finish and free its resources.

At this point, some other process will hold the highest resource and can also finish. In short, there exists a scenario in which all processes finish, so no deadlock is present. A minor variation of this algorithm is to drop the requirement that resources be acquired in strictly increasing sequence and merely insist that no process request a resource lower than what it is already holding. If a process initially requests 9 and 10, and then releases both of them, it is effectively starting all over, so there is no reason to prohibit it from now requesting resource 1.

Although numerically ordering the resources eliminates the problem of deadlocks, it may be impossible to find an ordering that satisfies everyone. When the resources include process table slots, disk spooler space, locked database records.

The various approaches to deadlock prevention are summarized in Table 4.1.

Table 4.1: Summary of Approaches to Deadlock Prevention

Condition	Approach
Mutual exclusion	Spool everything
Hold and wait	Request all resources initially
No preemption	Take resources away
Circular wait	Order resources numerically

4.7.   Research on Deadlocks

If ever there was a subject that was investigated mercilessly during the early days of operating systems, it was deadlocks. The reason for this is that deadlock detection is a nice little graph-theory problem that one mathematically inclined graduate student can get his jaws around and chew on for 3 or 4 years. All kinds of algorithms were devised, each one more exotic and less practical than the previous one. Most of that work has died out, but there are still papers being published on various aspects of deadlocks. These include runtime detection of deadlocks caused by incorrect use of locks and semaphores (Agarwal and Stoller, 2006; and Bensalem et al., 2006), preventing deadlocks among Java threads (Permandia et al., 2007; and Williams et al., 2005), dealing with deadlocks in networks (Jayasimha, 2003; Karol.et al, 2003; and Schafer et al., 2005), modeling deadlocks in dataflow systems (Zhou and Lee, 2006), and detecting dynamic deadlocks (Li et al., 2005) Levine (2003a, 2003b) compared different (and often contradictory) definitions of deadlock in the literature and came up with a classification scheme for them. She also took another look at the difference between deadlock prevention and deadlock avoidance (Levine, 2005). Recovery from deadlock is also being studied (David et al., 2007).

There is also some (theoretical) research on distributed deadlock detection, however. We will not treat that here because (1) it is outside the scope of this book, and (2) none of it is even remotely practical in real systems. Its main function seems to be keeping otherwise unemployed graph theorists off the streets.

4.8.   Summary

Deadlock is a potential problem in any operating system. It occurs when all the members of a set of processes are blocked waiting for an event that only other members of the set can cause. This situation causes all the processes to wait forever. Commonly the event that the processes are waiting for is the release of some resource held by another member of the set.

Another situation in which deadlock is possible is when a set of communicating processes are all waiting for a message and the communication channel is empty and no timeouts are pending.

Resource deadlock can be avoided by keeping track of which states are safe and which are unsafe. A safe state is one in which there exists a sequence of events that guarantee that all processes can finish. An unsafe state has no such guarantee. The banker's algorithm avoids deadlock by not granting a request if that request will put the system in an unsafe state.

Resource deadlock can be structurally prevented by building the system in such a way that it can never occur by design. For example, by allowing a process to hold only one resource at any instant the circular wait condition required for deadlock is broken. Resource deadlock can also be prevented by numbering all the resources, and making processes request them in strictly increasing order. Resource deadlock is not the only kind of deadlock. Communication deadlock is also a potential problem in some systems although it can often be handled by setting appropriate timeouts.

Livelock is similar to deadlock in that it can stop all forward progress, but it is technically different since it involves processes that are not actually blocked. Starvation can be avoided by a first-come, first-served allocation policy.

CHAPTER 5

FILE SYSTEMS

All computer applications need to store and retrieve information. While a process is running, it can store a limited amount of information within its own address space. However, the storage capacity is restricted to the size of the virtual address space. For some applications this size is adequate, but for others, such as airline reservations, banking, or corporate record keeping, it is far too small.

A second problem with keeping information within a process' address space is that when the process terminates, the information is lost. For many applications, (e.g., for databases), the information must be retained for weeks, months, or even forever. Having it vanish when the process using it terminates is unacceptable. Furthermore, it must not go away when a computer crash kills the process.

A third problem is that it is frequently necessary for multiple processes to access (parts of) the information at the same time. If we have an online telephone directory stored inside the address space of a single process, only that process can access it. The way to solve this problem is to make the information itself independent of any one process.

Thus we have three essential requirements for long-term information storage:

- It must be possible to store a very large amount of information.
- The information must survive the termination of the process using it.
- Multiple processes must be able to access the information concurrently.

5.1. Files

File is the visible aspect of the operating system. It also provides the means for online storage, as well as access to both data and programs belonging to the operating system and users of the system.

1) A collection of files where each storage corresponds to a related data.
2) A directory structure which organizes files and provides information about all the files in the system.
3) Partitions: These are used to separate logically or physically the large collections of directories.

A file is a collection of related information that is recorded on a secondary storage. A files usually represents programs (some and object) and data. Files may be in free–form like text files or may be formatted rigidly. This information in a file is defined by its creator and will have a defined structure according to its type.

For Example

1) A text–file is a sequence of characters organized into lines or pages
2) A source file is a sequences and functions and so on.

5.2. File Attributes

A file is named for the user's convenience and is referred to by its name. A name is usually a character string like test.c, test.f, etc. Attributes of a files, vary from one operating system to another but typically the attributes are:

1) Name: This will be usually is human readable form.
2) Type: This information is required in the systems which support different types.
3) Location: This is a pointer to a device and to the location of the file on that device.
4) Size: This gives information about, the current size of the file typically in bytes, words, blocks.
5) Protection: This is access–control information and controls reading, writing, executing and so on.
6) Time, data, user identification: This information is kept for the file's creation, last modification and last use.

The table 5.1 shows some of the possibilities, but other ones also exist. No existing system has all of these, but each one is present in some system.

Table 5.1: Some Possible File Attributes

Attribute	Meaning
Protection	Who can access the file and in what wav
Password	Password needed to access the file
Creator	ID of the person who created the file
Owner	Current owner
Read-only flag	0 for read/write; 1 for read only
Hidden flag	0 for normal; 1 for do not display in listings
System flag	0 for normal files; 1 for system file
Archive flag	0 for has been backed up; 1 for needs to be backed up
Key position	Offset of the key within each record
Key length	Number of bytes in the key field
Creation time	Date and time the file was created
Current size	Number of bytes in the file
Maximum size	Number of bytes the file may grow to

The first four attributes relate to the file's protection and tell who may access it and who may not. All kinds of schemes are possible, some of which we will study later. In some systems the user must present a password to access a file in wmcn case the password must be one of the attributes.

The flags are bits or short fields that control or enable some specific property Hidden files, for example, do not appear in listings of all the files. The archive flag is a bit that keeps track of whether the file has been backed up recently.

The backup program clears it, and the operating system sets it whenever a file is changed. In this way, the backup program can tell which files need backing up. The temporary flag allows a file to be marked for automatic deletion when the process that created it terminates. The record length, key position, and key length fields are only present in files whose records can be looked up using a key.

They provide the information required to find the keys. The various times keep track of when the file was created, most recently accessed, and most recently modified. These are useful for a variety of purposes. For example, a source file that has been modified after the creation of the corresponding object file needs to be recompiled. These fields provide the necessary information.

The current size tells how big the file is at present. Some old mainframe operating systems require the maximum size to be specified when the file is created, in order to let the operating system reserve the maximum amount of storage in advance. Workstation and personal computer operating systems are clever enough to do without this feature.

5.3.   File Access

Early operating systems provided only one kind of file access: sequential access. In these systems, a process could read all the bytes or records in a file in order, starting at the beginning, but could not skip around and read them out of order. Sequential files could be rewound, however, so they could be read as often as needed.

Sequential files were convenient when the storage medium was magnetic tape rather than disk. When disks came into use for storing files, it became possible to read the bytes or records of a file out of order, or to access records by key rather than by position. Files whose bytes or records can be read in any order are called random access files. E.g: Database management systems. They are required by many applications. Random access files are essential for many applications, for example, database systems. If an airline customer calls up and wants to reserve a seat on a particular flight, the reservation program must be able to access the record for that flight without having to read the records for thousands of other flights first.

Two methods can be used for specifying where to start reading. In the first one, every read operation gives the position in the file to start reading at. In the second one, a special operation, seek, is provided to set the current position. After a seek, the file can be read sequentially from the now-current position. The latter method is used in UNIX and Windows.

5.4.   File Operations

Files exist to store information and allow it to be retrieved later. Different systems provide different operations to allow storage and retrieval. Below is a discussion of the most common system calls relating to files.

Create: The file is created with no data. The purpose of the call is to announce that the file is coming and to set some of the attributes.

Delete: When the file is no longer needed, it has to be deleted to free up disk space. There is always a system call for this purpose.

Open: Before using a file, a process must open it. The purpose of the open call is to allow the system to fetch the attributes and list of disk addresses into main memory for rapid access on later calls.

Close: When all the accesses are finished, the attributes and disk addresses are no longer needed, so the file should be closed to free up internal table space. Many systems encourage this by imposing a maximum number of open files on processes. A disk is written in blocks, and closing a file forces writing of the file's last block, even though that block may not be entirely full yet.

Read: Data are read from file. Usually, the bytes come from the current position. The caller must specify how many data are needed and must also provide a buffer to put them in.

Write: Data are written to the file again, usually at the current position. If the current position is the end of the file, the file's size increases. If the current position is in the middle of the file, existing data are overwritten and lost forever.

Append: This call is a restricted form of write. It can only add data to the end of the file. Systems that provide a minimal set of system calls do not generally have append, but many systems provide multiple ways of doing the same thing, and these systems sometimes have append.

Seek: For random access files, a method is needed to specify from where to take the data. One common approach is a system call, seek, that repositions the file pointer to a specific place in the file. After this call has completed, data can be read from, or written to, that position.

Get attributes: Processes often need to read file attributes to do their work. For example, the UNIX make program is commonly used to manage software development projects consisting of many source files. When make is called, it examines the modification times of all the source and object files and arranges for the minimum number of compilations required to bring everything up to date. To do its job, it must look at the attributes, namely, the modification times.

Set attributes: Some of the attributes are user settable and can be changed after the file has been created. This system call makes that possible. The protection mode information is an obvious example. Most of the flags also fall in this category.

Rename: It frequently happens that a user needs to change the name of an existing file. This system call makes that possible. It is not always strictly necessary, because the file can usually be copied to a new file with the new name, and the old file then deleted.

5.5.   File Naming

Files are an abstraction mechanism. They provide a way to store information on the disk and read it back later. This must be done in such a way as to shield the user from the details of how and where the information is stored, and how the disks actually work. Probably the most important characteristic of any abstraction mechanism is the way the objects being managed are named, so we will start our examination of file systems with the subject of file naming. When a process creates a file, it gives the file a name. When the process terminates, the file continues to exist and can be accessed by other processes using its name.

The exact rules for file naming vary somewhat from system to system, but all current operating systems allow strings of one to eight letters as legal file names. Thus andrea, bruce, and cathy are possible file names. Frequently digits and special characters are also permitted, so names like 2, urgent! are often valid as well.

Many file systems support names as long as 255 characters. Some file systems distinguish between upper and lower case letters, whereas others do not. UNIX falls in the first category; MS-DOS falls in the second. Thus a UNIX system can have all of the following as three distinct files: maria, Maria, and MARIA. In MS-DOS, all these names refer to the same file. An aside on file systems is probably in order here. Windows 95 and Windows 98 both use the MS-DOS file system, called FAT-16, and thus inherit many of its properties, such as how file names are constructed.

Windows 98 introduced some extensions to FAT-16, leading to FAT-32, but these two are quite similar. In addition, Windows NT, Windows 2000, Windows XP, and WV support both FAT file systems, which are really obsolete now. These four NT-based operating systems have a native file system (NTFS) that has different properties (such as file names in Unicode). In this chapter, when we refer to the MS-DOS or FAT file systems, we mean FAT-16 and FAT-32 as used on Windows unless specified otherwise.

Many operating systems support two-part file names, with the two parts separated by a period, as in prog.c. The part following the period is called the file extension and usually indicates something about the file. In MS-DOS, for example, file names are 1 to 8 characters, plus an optional extension of 1 to 3 characters. In UNIX, the size of the extension, if any, is up to the user, and a file may even have two or more extensions, as in homepage.html.zip, where .html indicates a Web page in HTML and .zip indicates that the file (homepage.html) has been compressed using the zip program. Some of the more common file extensions and their meanings are shown in Table 5.2.

Table 5.2: Some Typical File Extensions

Extension	Meaning
file. bak	Back up file.
file. C	C source program
file. gif	CompuServe graphical Interchange Format Image.
file. h/p	Help file.
file. html	World wide web hyper text mark-up language document
file. JPEG	Still picture encoded with the JPEG standard
file. O	File object (compiler, output).
file. pdf	Portable document format file.
file. ps	Post script file.
file. txt	General text file.
file. zip	Compressed archive.

In some systems (e.g., UNIX), file extensions are just conventions and are not enforced by the operating system. A file named file.txt might be some kind of text file, but that name is more to remind the owner than to convey any actual information to the computer. On the other hand, a C compiler may actually insist that files it is to compile end in .c, and it may refuse to compile them if they do not.

Conventions like this are especially useful when the same program can handle several different kinds of files. The C compiler, for example, can be given a list of several files to compile and link together, some of them C files and some of them assembly language files. The extension then becomes essential for the compiler to tell which are C files, which are assembly files, and which are other files.

In contrast, Windows is aware of the extensions and assigns meaning to them. Users (or processes) can register extensions with the operating system and specify for each one which program "owns" that extension. When a user double clicks on a file name, the program assigned to its file extension is launched with the file as parameter. For example, double clicking onfile.doc starts Microsoft Word with file.doc as the initial file to edit.

5.6. File Types

In designing a file system and the entire operating system, one must consider whether the operating system must recognize and support the file types. One common approach used for implementing file types name.

Hence the file name is split into two parts

1) Name.
2) Extension, separated by a period.

Character as shown blow

File types	Extension	Function
Source code	.Pas, .C, .p, .ftt, etc	Source code in different Languages.

File types	Extension	Function
Object code	.obj, .o	Compiled, machine Languages not linked.

File types	Extension	Function
Executable	.exe, .com, .bin and so on	Really to run machine Languages program.

Figure 5.1: Characters

5.7. File System Management

The part of the operating system that deals with effective information management is called as file system management. The term file is used for anything that is stored in the secondary storage. A file could be a program, text files, word documents, image files, audio/video files etc. The file system management of the os deals with management these files and in providing a consistent mechanism for the user to access these files. The desirable feature of a file system are as follows:

1) Provide minimal input and output operation on the files to access the information stored in them.

2) Isolate the differences between the actual physical storage of these files and the one which the end user sees when he/she accesses these files.

The file system management of two well known file system, namely MS-DOS file system and UNIX file system, are discussed in this section.

MS-DOS File System

The file naming convention in DOS consists of logical drive, path and files name. The following examples would help in better understanding of above mentioned terms. Consider the following example shown in Figure suppose that JSC.doc is a file which is placed in a particular location, say C:|JSC |course material. Then c: refers to the logical drive name and C:|JSC | course material is called the path name. The path specifies the location in the logical drive where in the files is present. The path could be thought of as the route which one specifies to reach a particular destination. There could be multiple logical drives in an os; for example C:, D: etc.

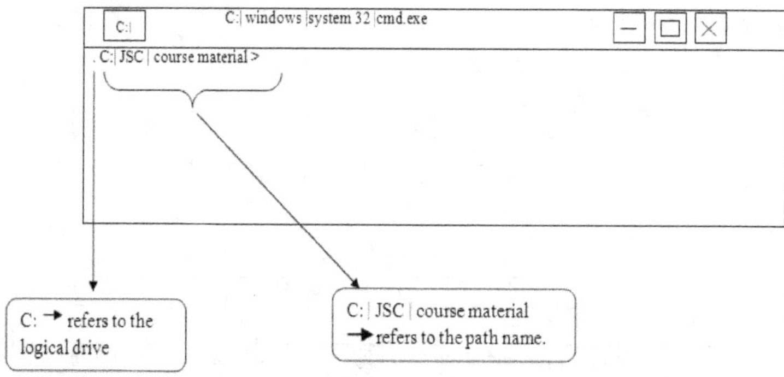

Figure 5.1: Example for File Naming Convention in MS-DOS

In the above example "JSC" and course material are called directories. A directory is a logical grouping of files. In other words a directory is a collection of files with is related to a user or an application. The files are organized on each logical drive within a hierarchical directory structure called a tree. A tree is a hierarchical data structure using a parent-child relationship to organize files. Refer to figure for an explanation on tree structure.

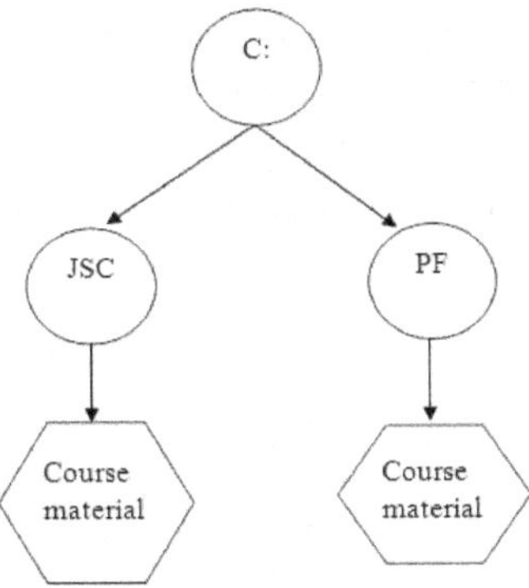

Figure 5.2: Example for a Tree Data Structure

Top of the directory is known as a root directory which holds numerous files and sub direction. In this example C: is the root directory and it has numerous files and sub-directories. The sub-directories shown are JSC and PF. Each of these sub directories further has sub-directories called course material.

File Organization in MS-Dos

This subsection deals with the organization of files in the hard disk in an Ms-Dos. The os allocates disk space based on the demand made by the user programs.

Here for the discussion of the structure of a hard disk. The hard disk is normally made up of multiple disk Platters. Disk platters are similar to a collection of compact disks pilled on top of each other. Normally, the hard disk is made up of three platters. The disk platters is divided into three platters. The disk platters is divided into circular recording units called tracks. The track is in turn subdivided into sectors. A sector can be considered to be the basic data storage unit in a hard disk. A number of sectors make a track and a number of tracks make a disk platter. The set of tracks across platters which have the same radius form a cylinder. So the hierarchy in terms of disk structures is that a number of sectors make up a track and a number of tracks made up a cylinder.

In Ms-Dos file system the disk space is normally allocated in units of a fixed size is called a cluster. A cluster is a collection of sectors. In other words a cluster is a multiple of sector size. Typical size of a cluster are 512, 1024, 2048, bytes. So any new file that is created will have a minimum space assigned to it which is nothing but one cluster. As more data is added to this file, it gets appended to the cluster and based on the further demand additional clusters are allocated for this file.

The clusters can be considered as synonyms with the paging technique which was discussed in memory management since there are multiple files in the system which could be accessed at any given point of time, the cluster allocated for these files may not sit in contiguous in the hard disk. Consider a situation where in a user creates a file, say file A and puts some data into it.

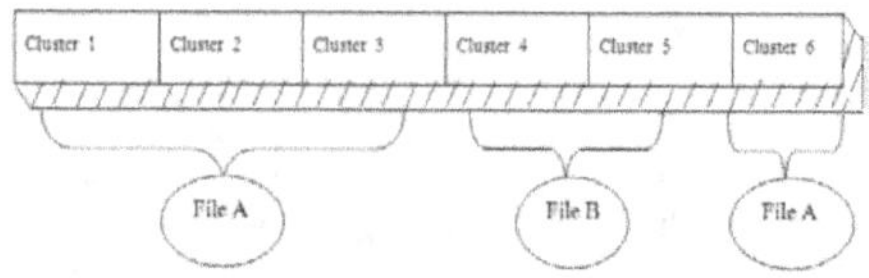

Figure 5.3: Example for Clustering Based File Structure

Three clusters are allocated to file A. Now this file is closed and another file, say file B is created and some data is put to this file. Two clusters are allocated to file B. Again when file A is opened to append some data a new cluster is not contiguous to the earlier clusters of file A.

Data Access in MS-Dos

To identify all the clusters of a particular file Ms-Dos uses a mechanism where the next cluster number in the sequence is stored in a table. This table is called the file allocation table (FAT). The FAT is similar to a table of contents that gives information about the clusters allocated to every file in the disk. The FAT is an array of 16 bit entries. The array index starts from 0. The entries in the array correspond to the cluster numbers of a file except for the first two entries of the FAT.

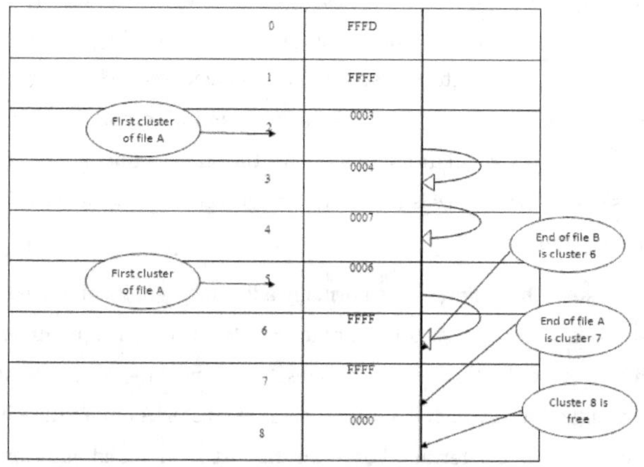

Figure 5.4 : File Allocation Table(FAT)

The first entry of the FAT which is FFFD. Identifies the disk type and the second entry which is FFFF indicates a value which signifies the last cluster of a file. The first cluster of file A is cluster 2. The FAT entry for index 2 is 0003 which indicates that the next cluster of file A is cluster 3 is 0004 which means cluster 4 is the next cluster. Following cluster 4 is cluster 7 in the sequence and from the FAT entry for index 7, which is FFFF, it is seen that cluster 7 is the last cluster of file A. Similarly the sequence of cluster for file B is cluster 6. Also a value of 0000 in the FAT indicates that a particular cluster is free. In the above diagram (File Allocation table) cluster 8 is free cluster. The FAT mechanism is also known as system of chained pointers as each entry is the FAT points to the next cluster number for a particular file there by forming a chain of pointers.

Volume Structure of the Disk in Ms-Dos

The term volume refers to the storage area in the secondary storage. A hard disk can have multiple volumes. The volume structure of a disk defines the way in which disk defines the in which disk is organized. In Ms-Dosos the volume structure of the disk has the following.

1) Boot Sector

The Boot sector contains all information about the disk characteristics. Some of these disk characteristics are the disk manufacturer's name, version and the allocation details like the number of tracks. Per cluster and the number of FATS. (In Ms-Dosos a number of copies of the FAT are Maintained so that it can be used if the main. FATS gets corrupted). The boot sector also contains an important program called the bootstrap loader. The bootstrap loader is the one of the first program which gets executed when the computer is switched on and the bootstrap loader loads the os from the disk to the main memory.

2) FAT

The file allocation table is part of the volume structure of the disk.

3) Additional FAT(S)

Duplicate copies of the FAT are stored in the disk which gets updated along with the main FAT. The duplicate copies are used if the main FAT. The duplicate copies used if the main FAT gets computed.

4) Root Directory

It is a special kind of directory which has a fixed position in the disk and also the size of the root is fixed. The os programs normally reside in the root directory.

5) File Space

Relates to rest of the disk which is used for files and sub-directories.

MS-Dos Booting Process

Whenever the computer is switched on, a piece of program called BIOS performs a test to check if the hardware components are functioning properly. This test is called power on self test (POST). After performing the POST the BIOS starts performing the Root booting process by reading through the boot sector in the hard disk loading the bootstrap loader into the Main memory and executing it.

The bootstrap loader now locates the Ms-Dos operating system files in the root directory and loads them into main memory and executes them which in turn makes the operating system function.

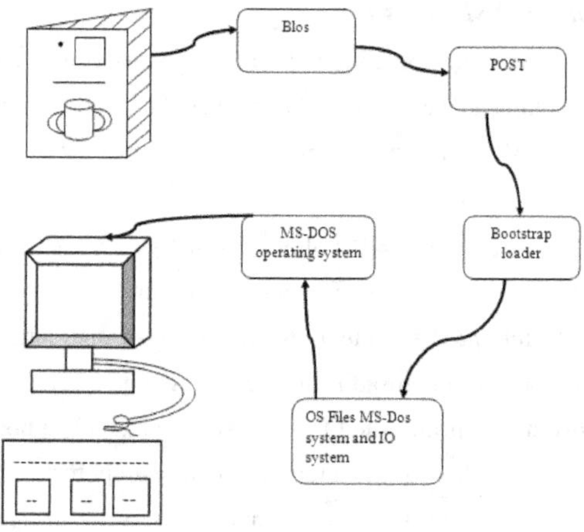

Figure 5.5: MS–DOS Booting Process

Unix File System

In Unixos the Hard Disk can be divided into Multiple file systems. Recall that a file system is the structure in which files are organized. Analogous to clusters in Ms-Dos, UNIX allocates disk space in terms of blocks. The block size is a multiple of 512 bytes. A file system in UNIX consist of a sequence of logical blocks. There is one compulsory file system in UNIX which is called the Root file system. The remaining file systems are optional and are left to the choice of the Administrator. The file system in UNIX is different to that of Ms-Dos. UNIX file system is hierarchical. At the top of the hierarchy is the root file system which acts as parent to the remaining three file systems, namely file system 2, file system 3 and file system 4.

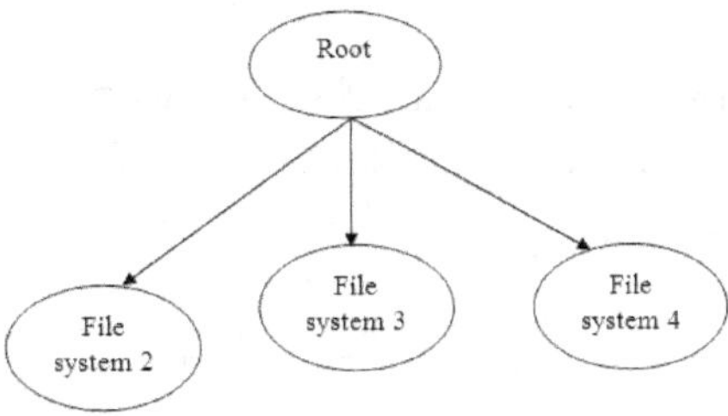

Figure 5.6: UNIX File System Hierarchy

5.8.   File Organization in Unix

The disk storage in UNIX can be viewed as one which has three components, namely:

1)   Directory Entry Table.

2)   Inode block.

3)   Data blocks.

Directory Entry Table

Every directory in UNIX has a directory entry table which has the following information every file in that directory.

1)   *Name of the file.

2)   *A pointer to a block which contains.

The detailed information about the file. This block is called node block.

Inode Block

A data structure called inode block is used for describing every file in unix. The node inode block contains information about the file. Every file is UNIX has an inode block associated to it. This is inode block is identified by a unique number inode block is identified by a unique number called the inode number which is associated to every file. The following are some of the important information which the inode block contain for every file.

1)   Type of the file.

2)   Location of the file.

3)   Size of the file.

4)   Last modified time of the file.

5)   Last accessed time of the file.

6)   A set of pointers to a block which contain the actual data of the file.

Data Blocks

The data blocks are the one which contains the actual data. These data blocks are allocated by UNIX whenever some data is written to a file. An example of the disk storage for two files (File 1, File 2) is shown in figure.

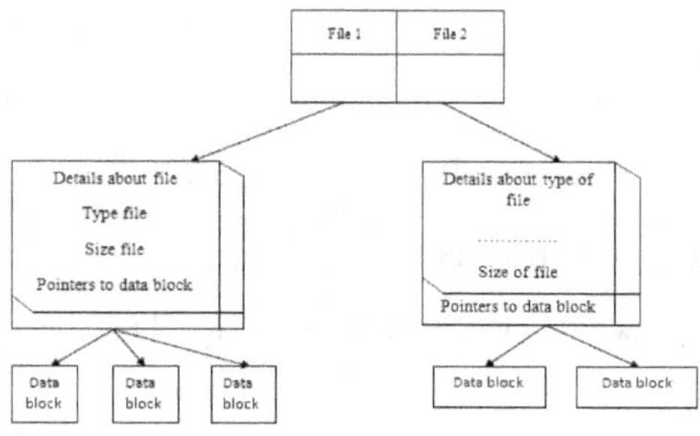

Figure 5.7: Disk Storage in UNIX

Data Access in UNIX

The mode block for every file has an array of thirteen pointers. The first 10 elements of the array of pointers are called direct pointer. These element point to the address of a data block in the hard disk. Whenever a file is created a data block is allocated to the file store the data and also the first position of the array. The first direct pointer has the address of the first data block that was allocated. As and when the size of a file increases, the os allocated data blocks to it and stores the address of these data block in the renaming direct pointers in the inode block . So, if ten data blocks are allocated to a file then the address os these data blocks will be stored in the ten direct pointers of the inode block of this file. This would mean that the size of the file is 512*10=5120 bytes.

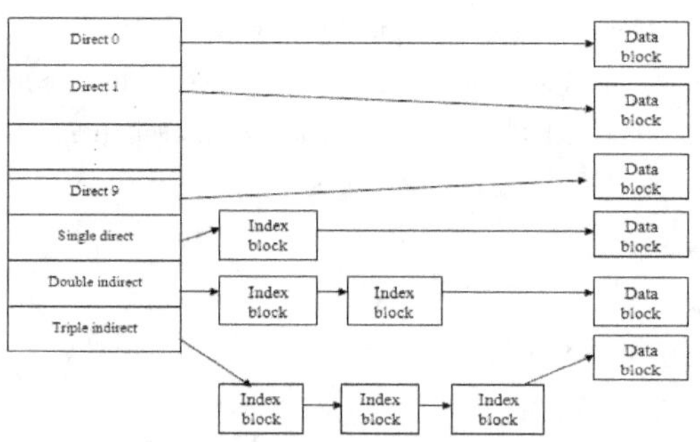

Figure 5.8 : Inode Pointer Structure

When the size of the file grow beyond 5120 bytes, then the UNIX OS uses the 11th pointer called the single direct pointer, to get the address of the data blocks. This single indirect pointers does not directly point to a data block, instead it points to a block called index block which is 512 bytes of size.

This index block is an array of pointers. Since each pointer occupies 4bytes, the number of such pointers possible for the index block is total size divided by the size of one pointer which 512/4=128. So the index block is divided init an array of 128 pointers. Each of these 128 pointers points to a data blocks of 512 bytes. This is equivalent to 138 data blocks.

Now of the size of the file grows beyond 70656 bytes the UNIX uses the 12th pointer, called the double indirect pointer, to get the address of the data blocks. The double indirect pointer points to an index block of 512 bytes of size. This index block of the 128 pointer which in turn point to the data blocks. In the way maximum size of the file that could be addressed using double indirect pointer would be 128*128*512=8388608 bytes. Hence the total file size that could be addressed using all the ten direct pointers, the single indirect pointer and the double indirect pointer is 70656+8388608=8459264 bytes. This equivalent to 16522 data blocks. If the size of the file grows beyond 8459264 bytes then UNIX the 13th pointer, called triple indirect pointer, which is used to get the address of the data blocks. The triple indirect pointer to get the address of the data blocks. The triple indirect pointer pointes to an index block of 128 pointers each of which points to another index block of 128 pointers. Each of the 128 pointers in the second index block again point to an index block of 128 pointers each of which in turn points to a data block. So the maximum size of the file that could be addressed using the triple indirect. Pointer would be 128*128*128*512=1073741824 bytes. Hence the total file size that could be addressed using all the ten direct pointers, the single indirect pointer; the double indirect pointer is 8459264 + 1073741824 = 1082201088 bytes. This is equivalent to 2113674 data blocks. If the size of the file grows beyond this size the UNIX has a provision include the fourth indirect pointer and so on.

Volume Structure of the Disk in UNIX

The volume structure if UNIX is different from that of MS-DOS. Recall that UNIX allows multiple file system to exist in the same hard disk. Every file system in UNIX has the following layout.

1) Boot block
2) Super block
3) Inode block
4) Data block

Boot Block

The boot block contains the boot strap loader which is copied into the main memory when the computer is powered on. The boot strap loader is the first program which gets executed when the computer is switched on, which in turn loads the UNIX OS into the main memory. The boot block is analogous to the boot sector in MS-DOS.

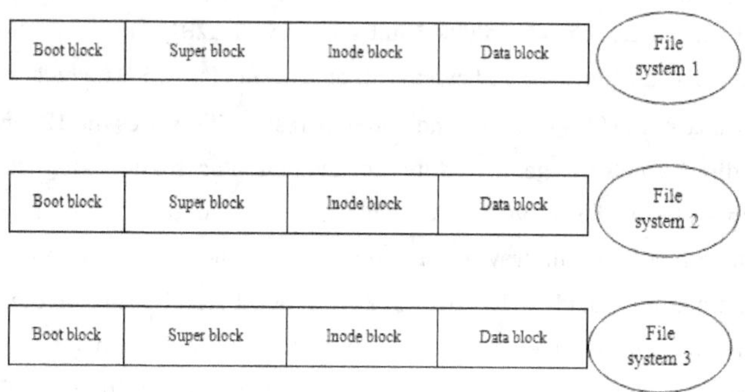

Figure 5.9: Volume Structure of UNIX File System

The figure shows three file systems as part of a disk in UNIX and all the three have the boot block.

Super Block

The super block has the complete summary of the file system. It describes the states of the file system by maintain the following information.

1) Size of the file system.
2) List of free inode blocks.
3) List of free data blocks.
4) Size of the disk blocks.

Inode Block

The Inode block following the super block and it has a unique record, the inode, for every file in the file system. The inode gives all the information about the file and the disk layout of the file. The inode for every file is identified and accessed by a number called the inode number. Some of the important information.

1) Type of the file.
2) Location of the file.

3) Size of the file .

4) Last modified time of the file.

5) Last accessed time of the file .

6) A set of pointers to a block which contains that actual data of that file. This block is called the data block.

Data Block

The data block contains only data. The information about which data block corresponds to which file is maintained in the inode block.

5.9. File Permission

Dos is not a multi-user system. The security in terms of file permission is very limited in nature. On a system with many users sharing the files, is very important to keep a few files private, UNIX is a multi-user ,multitasking, multiprocessing operating system.

In UNIX every user has a username and belongs to one group. For example, username could be Raja belonging to group called Aug 05. There could be others users in the same group. As well there could be many other groups of similar kind.

The files belonging to user Raja could be allowed to be accessed by other group members on even the members of other groups, If the owner (Raja) is willing to do so.

A file could be accessible to read, write or execute. In execute mode the executable files can be executed. The read, write and execute permission could be given to a file in such a way that only the owner can u se them accordingly, or permission could be given to the entire group or members of other groups.

Consider a case where the owner of the file wants to give read, write and execute permission the all members in group and the others as well, then the permission set will be as shown figure 5.10(a). Similarly the situation where in the owner wants to keep all the access permissions to himself but restrict the group and others to read only is shown in figure 5.10(b). Figure 5.10(c) shows a situation where in all kinds of access permission are given to owner but read and write to group and no access permission of any kind is given to the others.

File permission could also be represented in terms of numbers as well. Read is given a value of 4, write is equal to 2 and execute is equal to 1. So in the case of Figure 5.10(a) where in the users file has Read Write Execute (=4+2+1=7) permission for owner, group and other, we can represent the permission for this file as 777. Similarly the file permission for the case in Figure 5.10 (b) is 744. Figure 5.10(c) is 760.

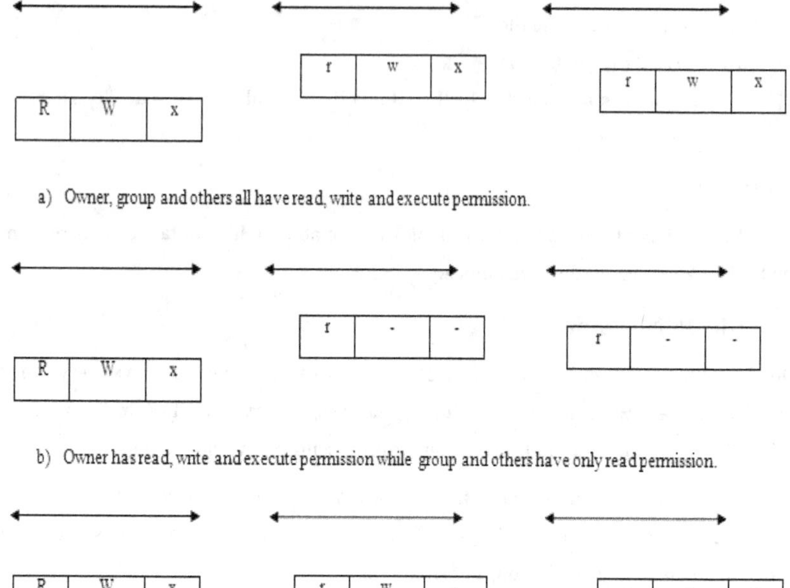

Figure 5.10: File Access Calculation

5.10. New Technology File System (NTFS)

NTFS is a file system used by windows NT and its descendants (windows 2000 and windows-xp). This is completely different from FAT file system used in MS-DOS and early version of windows. NTFS has several improvements over the FAT like improved support to store the information of the files and the data structure so as to improve the performance, reliability, security and optimal disk space utilization. Some of the features of the NTFS file system are:

1) Security and access control.
2) Size of the files.
3) Recovery/Reliability.
4) Long file names.

Security and Access Control

Like in UNIX, this file system implements built in faculty for controlling access to the files and folders in the hard disk. This is a very important feature which was not so inherently built in FAT based file system.

Size of the Files

NTFS supports large file and virtually any numbers of files in the hard disk. Unlike in FAT the performance does not degrade with large volume of data access. In FAT, file system the FAT's would occupy a large amount of disk space themselves. The NTFS uses a different approach to allocate space to the files, thus using disk space efficiently.

Recovery/Reliability

NTFS implements features to recover from problems without any loss of data. In the event of a system crash, the file system design prevents corruption of data.

Long File Names

NTFS allows file names to be of 255 characters in length. In FAT the limitation was 8 characters for filename and 3 for extension names (Example: myfile.doc).

Overview of the Partition Structure

NTFS divides disk space into clusters as in case of the FAT file system. NTFS supports almost all sizes of cluster from 512 bytes to 64kbytes. But 4kbytes is considered to be the standard one. The NTFS is logically divided into two parts as shown in figure 5.11:

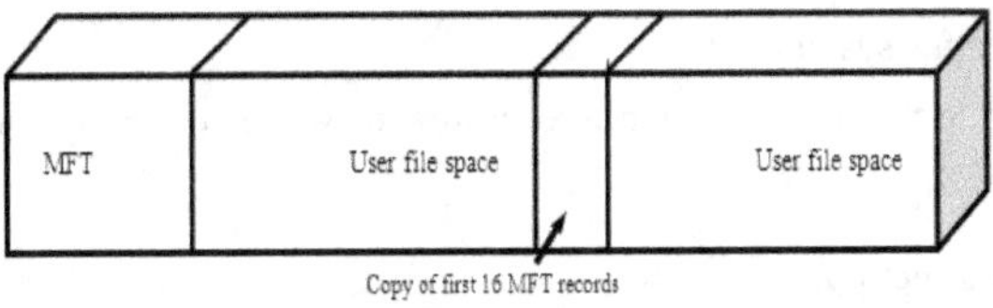

Figure 5.11: NFTS Partition Structure

The first part in the partition structure is called the Meta File Table or MFT. This holds the information about the other files called the metadata or the metafiles. The other part of this structure is used for the actual user data files. The MFT contains entries that describes all system files, user files and directories. Each MFT entry is given a number. The first sixteen entries in MFT correspond to the system files including #0 which describes the MFT itself. The users files and directories start at #25.

A copy of the first sixteen MFT entries is duplicated exactly at the middle of the user file space. The detailed discussion on the NTFS is beyond the scope of the discussion and is also the proprietary format of Microsoft.

Limitations of NTFS

1) The file encryption is not built in NTFS and hence one can boot through the MS-DOS or any other operating system and use low level disk editing utility to view data stored on a NTFS volume. NTFS 5 the enhanced version of NTFS address this issue.
2) For disk volumes of loss than 400MB, the overhead becomes too large.
3) Formatting floppy disks is not possible on NTFS.

5.11. Directory Structure

The file system in a computer can be very costly. In order to manage such entries data, file have to be organized. To keep tracks of files, file system normally has directories or folders, which in many systems, are themselves files. A directory can be viewed as a symbol table that translate file names into their directory entries while considering a particular directory structure, the operations that are to be performed on a directory must be kept in mind. These operations to be considered are:

1) Search for a file.
2) Create a file.
3) Delete a file.
4) List a directory.
5) Rename a file.
6) Traverse the file system.

In order to define the logical structure of a directory, the common structure used are as follows:

1) Single level directory.
2) Two level directory.
3) Tree structure directory.
4) Acyclic–graph directory.
5) General–graph directory.

Single–Level Directory

This is the simplest structure. All the files in this structure are contained in the same directory which becomes easy to understand and support. The simplest form of directory system is having one directory containing all the files. Sometimes it is called the root directory, but since it is the only one, the name does not matter much. This structure has limitations like when the number of files increases or when there is more than one user, since all the files are in the same directory. They must have unique names. Suppose if there are two users who make their files by the same name, then the unique name rule is violated and also with the increase in number of files. It is very difficult to recognize the filenames.

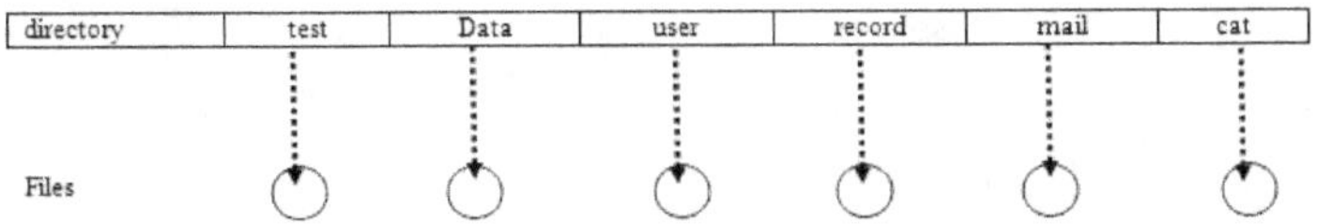

Figure 5.12: Single Level Directory

Two Level Directory

To overcome this disadvantage of a single level directory structure, that is the confusion of file names between different users, create a separate directory for each user. In this structure, each user has their own User File Directory (UFD). Each UFD has similar structure, but lists the files of only a single user. When a user Job starts or a user logs in, the system Master File Directory (MFD) is searched. MFD is indexed by the username or account number and each entry points to the LFD for that user as shown below. When a user refers to a particular file, only his own UFD is searched. So different users may have files with the same name, as long as all the filenames within each UFD are unique. A two level directory structure is shown in Fig:

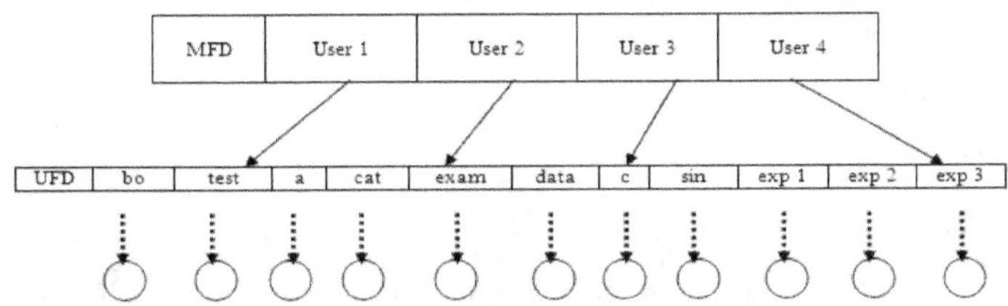

Figure 5.13 : Two Level Directory

Tree Structure Directory

The tree will have a root directory and every file in the system will have a unique path name. It is the path from root through all the sub directories to a specified file.

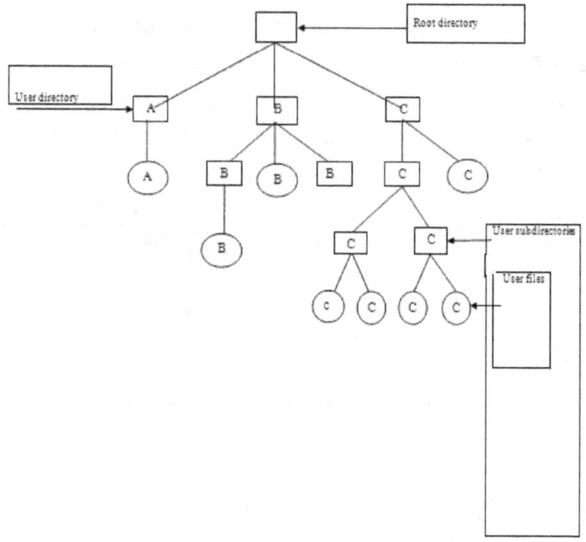

Figure 5.14: A Tree Structure Directory

A directory or sub directory contains a set of files or subdirectories. A directory is another file. All the directories will have the same internal format. One bit in each directory entry defines the entry as either a file (0) or as a subdirectory (1) special system calls will be available in the system to create and delete directories. Normally each user will have a current directory shown the Figure: Tree structured directory.

The path names can be of two types:

1) Absolute
2) Relative

Absolute Path

An absolute path name begins at root and follows a path down to a specified file, giving the directory names the path.

Relative Path

A relative path name defines a path from current directory.

For example ; if the current directory is root / spell / mail, then absolute path is root / spell / mail /exp / obj and relative path may be prt / obj.

In order to delete a directory, in this directory structure, first all the files under that directory must be deleted, that is, it must be made empty. E –MS-DOS.

Acyclic Graph Directories

This directory structure is used in a situation where a common sub directory should be shared. A shared directory or files will exist in the file system in two places at once with a shared file, there will be only one actual file, so any changes made by one user should be visible to another immediately. A tree structure prohibits the files or directory sharing. An cyclic graph structure allows directories to share subdirectories and files as shown in Fig:

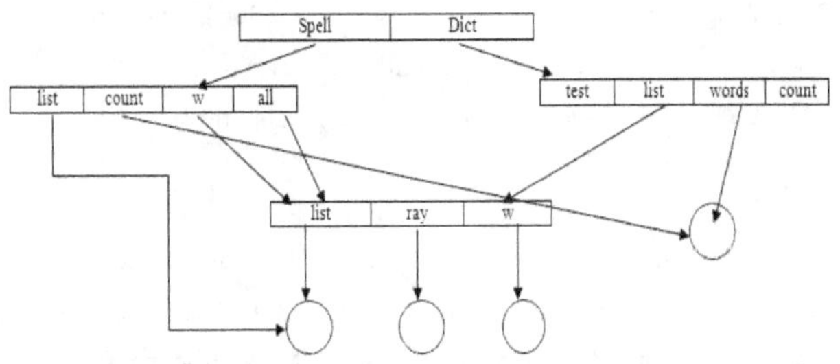

Figure 5.15 : Cyclic Graph Directories

Shared files and subdirectories can be implemented in different ways. Ex:44 UNIX first create a new directory entry called LINK. A link is a pointer to another file or subdirectory. A link may be implemented as an absolute or relative path name. When any reference to a file is made, the directory is searched. The directory entry is marked as a link and the name of the read file is given. Acyclic graph structure is more flexible than tree structure, but more complex.

5.12. Research on File Systems

File systems have always attracted more research than other parts of the operating system and that is still the case. While standard file systems are fairly well understood, there is still quite a bit of research going on about optimizing buffer cache management (Burnett et al., 2002; Ding et al, 2007; Gnaidy et al, 2004; Kroeger and Long, 2001; Pai et al., 2000; and Zhou et al., 2001). Work is going on about new kinds of Fde systems, such as user-level file systems (MazieTes, 2001), flash fde systems (Gal et al., 2005), journaling file systems (Prabhakaran et al., 2005; and Stein et al., 2001), versioning file systems (Cornell et al., 2004), peer-to-peer file systems (Muthitacharoen et al., 2002) and others. The Google file system is also unusual due to its great fault tolerance (Ghemawat et al., 2003). Different ways of finding things in file systems are also of interest (Padioleau and Ridoux, 2003).

Another area that has been getting attention is provenance—keeping track of the history of the data, including where they came from, who owns them, and how they has been transformed (Muniswarmy-Reddy et al., 2006; and Shah et al., 2007). This information can be used in a variety of ways. Making backups is still getting some attention, too (Cox et ai., 2002; and Rycroft, 2006), as is the related topic of recovery (Keeton et al., 2006). Related to backups is keeping data around and usable for decades (Baker et al., 2006; Maniatis et al., 2003). Reliability and security are also far from solved problems (Greenan and Miller, 2006; Wires and Feeley, 2007; Wright et al., 2007; and Yang et al., 2006). And finally performance has always been a research topic and still is (Caudill and Gavrikovska, 2006; Chiang and Huang, 2007; Srein, 2006; Wang et al., 2006a; and Zhang and Ghose, 2007).

5.13. Summary

When seen from the outside, a file system is a collection of files and directories, plus operations on them. Files can be read and written, directories can be created and destroyed, and files can be moved from directory to directory. Most modern file systems support a hierarchical directory system in which directories may have subdirectories and these may have sub subdirectories ad infinitum.

When seen from the inside, a file system looks quite different. The file system designers have to be concerned with how storage is allocated, and how the system keeps track of which block goes with which file. Possibilities include contiguous files, linked lists, file allocation tables, and i-nodes. Different systems have different directory structures. Attributes can go in the directories or somewhere else (e.g., an i-node). File system performance is important and can be enhanced in several ways, including caching, read ahead, and carefully placing the blocks of a file close to each other. Log-structured file systems also improve performance by doing writes in large units. Examples of file systems include ISO 9660, MS-DOS, and UNIX These differ in many ways, including how they keep track of which blocks go with which file, directory structure, and management of free disk space.

CHAPTER 6

DEVICE AND POWER MANAGEMENT

6.1. Input and Output Devices

The control of devices connected to the computer is a major concern of operating-system designers. Because I/O devices vary so widely in their function and speed (consider a mouse, a hard disk, and a CD-ROM jukebox), varied methods are needed to control them. These methods form the I/O subsystem of the kernel, which separates the rest of the kernel from the complexities of managing I/O devices.

I/O-device technology exhibits two conflicting trends. On one hand; we see increasing standardization of software and hardware interfaces. This trend helps us to incorporate improved device generations into existing computers and operating systems. On the other hand, we see an increasingly broad variety of I/O devices. Some new devices are so unlike previous devices that it is a challenge to incorporate them into our computers and operating systems. This challenge is met by a combination of hardware and software techniques. The basic I/O hardware elements, such as ports, buses, and device controllers, accommodate a wide variety of I/O devices. To encapsulate the details and oddities of different devices, the kernel of an operating system is structured to use device-driver modules. The device drivers present a uniform device access interface to the I/O subsystem, much as system calls provide a standard interface between the application and the operating system.

6.2. I/O Channels, Interrupts and Interrupt Handling

Recall, that a database is used to transfer data from one part of the computer to another. In order to overcome the disparity in speed of the operations between the I/O devices and the CPU a separate channel is maintained for the communication between the I/O devices and the computer. This cannel is called the I/O bus system or the I/O channel. The initiation and the completion of an I/O request between the CPU and the I/O channel is done by means of an interrupt. An interrupt is a hardware facility which causes the CPU to suspend its work, save the context of the currently executing process and send appropriate request to I/O devices. The CPU oversees the data transfer and sets appropriate status bit as and when required.

Once the I/O device has completed servicing this request, it sends an this device. The act of causing the CPU to suspend its work, save the context of the currently executing process and send appropriate requests to the I/O device is called interrupt handling routine. There are different kinds of interrupts like the peripheral interrupt, error interrupt etc which are classified based on their priority. A peripheral interrupt has the highest priority when compared to the other hardware interrupts. After a CPU initiates an I/O request it is necessary for the CPU to get involved in the data transfer during an I/O operation.

6.3.   Direct Memory Access (DMA)

No matter whether a CPU does or does not have memory-mapped I/O, it needs to address the device controllers to exchange data with them. The CPU can request data from an I/O controller one byte at a time but doing so wastes the CPU's time, so a different scheme, called DMA (Direct Memory Access) is often used. The operating system can only use DMA if the hardware has a DMA controller, which most systems do. Sometimes this controller is integrated into disk controllers and other controllers, but such a design requires a separate DMA controller for each device.

More commonly, a single DMA controller is available (e.g., on the parent board) for regulating transfers to multiple devices, often concurrently. No matter where it is physically located, the DMA controller has access to the system bus independent of the CPU, as shown in Fig. 6.1. It contains several registers that can be written and read by the CPU. These include a memory address register, a byte count register, and one or more control registers. The control registers specify the I/O port to use, the direction of the transfer (reading from the I/O device or writing to the I/O device), the transfer unit (byte at a time or word at a time), and the number of bytes to transfer in one burst.

To explain how DMA works, let us first look at how disk reads occur when DMA is not used. First the disk controller reads the block (one or more sectors) from the drive serially, bit by bit, until the entire block is in the controller's internal buffer. Next, it computes the checksum to verify that no read errors have occurred. Then the controller causes an interrupt. When the operating system starts running, it can read the disk block from the controller's buffer a byte or a word at a time by executing a loop, with each iteration reading one byte or word from a controller device register and storing it in main memory.

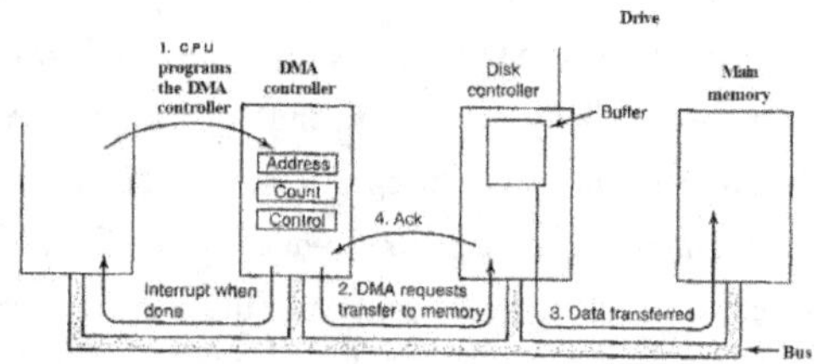

Figure 6.1: Operation of a DMA Transfer

When DMA is used, the procedure is different. First the CPU programs the DMA controller by setting its registers so it knows what to transfer where (step 1 in Fig. 6.1). It also issues a command to the disk controller telling it to read data from the disk into its internal buffer and verify the checksum. When valid data are in the disk controller's buffer, DMA can begin. The DMA controller initiates the transfer by issuing a read request* over the bus to the disk controller (step 2). This read request looks like any other read request, and the disk controller does not know or care whether it came from the CPU or from a DMA controller.

Typically, the memory address to write to is on the bus' address lines so when the disk controller fetches the next word from its internal buffer, it knows where to write it. The write to memory is another standard bus cycle (step 3). When the write is complete, the disk controller sends an acknowledgement signal to the DMA controller, also over the bus (step 4). The DMA controller then increments the memory address to use and decrements the byte count. If the byte count is still greater than 0, steps 2 through 4 are repeated until the count reaches 0. At that time, the DMA controller interrupts the CPU to let it know that the transfer is now complete. When the operating system starts up, it does not have to copy the disk block to memory; it is already there.

DMA controllers vary considerably in their sophistication. The simplest ones handle one transfer at a time, as described above. More complex ones can be programmed to handle multiple transfers at once. Such controllers have multiple sets of registers internally, one for each channel. The CPU starts by loading each set of registers with the relevant parameters for its transfer. Each transfer must use a different device controller. After each word is transferred (steps 2 through 4) in Fig. 6.1, the DMA controller decides which device to service next.

It may be set up to use a round-robin algorithm, or it may have a priority scheme design to favor some devices over others. Multiple requests to different device controllers may be pending at the same time, provided that there is an unambiguous way to tell the acknowledgements apart. Often a different acknowledgement line on the bus is used for each DMA channel for this reason.

Many buses can operate in two modes: word-at-a-time mode and block mode. Some DMA controllers can also operate in either mode. In the former mode, the operation is as described above: the DMA controller requests for the transfer of one word and gets it. If the CPU also wants the bus, it has to wait. The mechanism is called cycle stealing because the device controller sneaks in and steals an occasional bus cycle from the CPU once in a while, delaying it slightly. In block mode, the DMA controller tells the device to acquire the bus, issue a series of transfers, then release the bus. This form of operation is called burst mode. It is more efficient than cycle stealing because acquiring the bus takes time and multiple words can be transferred for the price of one bus acquisition. The down side to burst mode is that it can block the CPU and other devices for a substantial period of time if a long burst is being transferred.

6.4.   Software Interrupts

Software interrupts are Programmed interrupts. Recall that hardware interrupts are a special kind of device which provides the interrupt facility. Operating Systems provide the facility where in Programs (software) can act as interrupt. In what scenarios would these software interrupts used?

Consider an application Program that is being executed by a user. Whenever the application Program requires a service from the OS like reading data from the disk, a software interrupt also called as trap is generated which will save the current state of the application Program and invoke the file manager of the OS to provide the appropriate service. Once the data is read into memory the software interrupt restores back the current state of the application program so that it could continue from where it was interrupted. The control C-key which is normally used to send some kind of interrupt signal is also a software interrupt.

6.5.   Structure of an I/O System

Whenever an application Program requires any kind of I/O it sends a request to the I/O control System (IOCS). The I/O control system is a set of Programs which is part of the operating systems. The tasks of the I/O control system is to accept I/O request from application programs, do the initial Processing, validation of requests and to route the request to the appropriate device. The application requests are conveyed to the IOCS by means of software interrupts. The IOCS in turn sends these requests to device drivers which are software modules whose task is to convert the application program request, also called the logical request, into commands that the device can understand. In most of the cases each device has a separate device driver. The device driver sends these device specific requests to the device controller through the I/O bus.

Device controllers are hardware devices which control the devices. The device controller gets this request serviced by the hardware and routes the I/O response back to application program through the device driver and I/O control system.

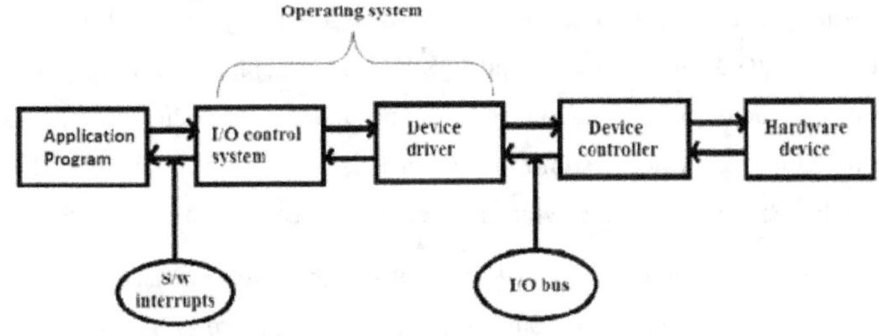

Figure 6.2: Structure of I/O System

6.6.   Power Management

Power management is back in the spotlight for several reasons, and the operating system is playing a role here. Power is a big issue is a battery–powered computers, including notebooks, laptops and web pads, among others. The heart of the problem is that batteries cannot hold enough charge to last very long, a few hours at most. There are two general approaches in reducing energy consumption. The first one is for the operating system to turn off parts of the computer when they are not in use because a device that is off uses little or no energy. The second one is for the application program to use less energy, possibly degrading the quality of the user experience, in order to stretch out–battery time.

6.6.1. Hardware Issues

Batteries come in two general types:

- Disposable.
- Rechargeable.

Disposable

Disposable batteries can be used to run handheld devices, but do not have enough energy to power laptop computers with large bright screens.

Rechargeable

A rechargeable battery, in contrast, can store enough energy to power a laptop for a few hours. Nickel cadmium batteries used to dominate here, but they gave way to nickel metal hydride batteries, which last longer and do not pollute the environment quite as badly when they are eventually discarded. Lithium ion batteries are even better, and may be recharged without first being fully drained, but their capacities are also severely limited.

The general approach most computer vendors take to battery conservation is to design the CPU, memory and I/O devices to have multiple states: on, sleeping hibernating, and off. To use the device, it must be on. When the device will is not needed for a short time, it can be put to sleep, which reduces energy consumption when it is not expected to needed for a longer interval it can be made to hibernate, which reduces energy consumption even more.

The trade off here is that getting a device out of hibernation often takes more time and energy than getting it out of sleep state. Finally, when a device is off, it does nothing and consumes no power. Not all devices have all these states, but when they do, it is up to the operating system to manage the state transitions at the right moments.

6.6.2. *Operating System Issues*

The operating system plays a key role in energy management. It controls all the devices, so it must decide what to shut down and when to shut it down.

If it shuts down a device and that device is needed again quickly, there may be an annoying delay while it is restarted. On the other hand, if it waits too long to shut down a device, energy is wasted for nothing.

The Display

The highest item in everyone's energy budget is the display. To get a bright sharp image, the screen must be backlit and that takes substantial energy. Many operating systems attempt to save energy here by shutting down the display when there has been no activity for some number of minutes. Often the user can decide what the shut down interval is, pushing the trade–off between frequent blanking of the screen and using the battery up quickly back to the user.

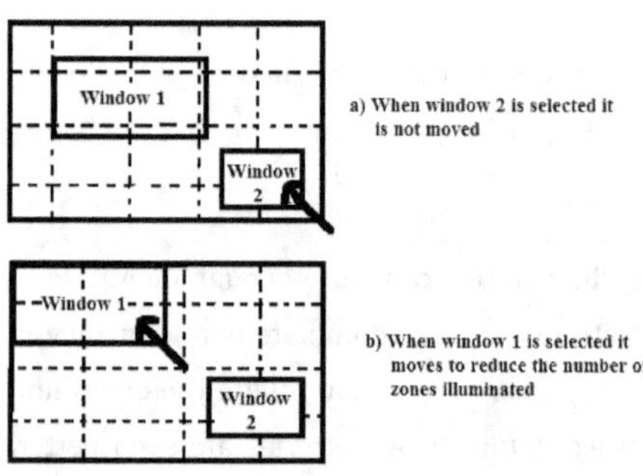

Figure 6.3: Window/Display

When the user moves the cursor to window 1, the zones for window 2 can be darkened and the zones behind window 1 can be turned on. However, because window 1 straddles 9 zones, more power is needed. If the window manager can sense of what is happening, it can automatically move window 1 to fit into four zones, with a kind of snap–to–zone action as shown in fig 6.3. To achieve this reduction from 9/16 of full power to 4/16 of full power, the windows manager has to understand power management or be capable of accepting instructions from some other piece of the system that does. Even more sophisticated would be the ability to partially illuminate a window that was not completely full.

The Hard Disk

It takes substantial energy to keep it spinning at high speed, even if there are no accesses. Many computers, especially laptops, spin the disk down after a certain number of minutes of activity. Unfortunately a stopped disk is hibernating rather than sleeping because it takes quite a few seconds to spin it up again, which causes noticeable delays for the user. In addition, restarting the disk consumes considerable extra energy. As a consequence, every disk has a characteristic time, Td that is its break–even point often in the range 5 to 15 sec. Suppose that the next disk access is expected to sometime t in the future. If t < Td, it takes less energy to keep the disk spinning rather than spin it down and then spin it up so quickly.

If t < Td, the energy saved makes it worth spinning the disk down and up again mush later if a good prediction could be made, the operating system could make good shutdown predictions and save energy. In practice, most systems are conservative and only spin down the disk after a few minutes of inactivity.

Another way to save disk energy is to have a substantial disk cache in RAM. If a needed block is in the cache has an idle disk does not have to be restarted to satisfy the read, similarly, if a write to the disk can be buffered in the cache, a stopped disk does not have to restarted just to handle the write. The disk can remain off until cache fills up or a read miss happens.

The CPU

The CPU can also be managed to save energy. A laptop CPU can be put to sleep in software, reducing power usage to almost zero. The only thing it can do in this state is wake up when an interrupt occurs. Therefore, whenever the CPU goes idle, either waiting for I/O or because there is no work to do, it goes to sleep. On many computers, there is a relationship between CPU voltage, clock cycle, and power usage. The CPU voltage can often be reduced in software which saves energy but also reduces the clock cycle. Since power consumed is proportional to the square of the voltage, cutting the voltage in half makes the CPU about half as fast but as 1/4power.

The Memory

Two possible options exist for saving energy with the memory.

Cache can be flushed and then switched off. It can always be reloaded from main memory with no loss of information the reloaded can be done dynamically and quickly, so turning off the cache is entering a sleep state. Amore drastic option is to write the contents of main memory to the disk, then switch off the main memory itself. When the main memory is cut off, the CPU either has to be shut off as well or has to execute out of ROM. If CPU is cut off, the interrupt that wakes it up has to cause it to jump to code in a ROM so the memory can be reloaded before being used.

Wireless Communication

One of the major issues in power management is Wireless Communication. Here the radio transmitter and receiver required are often first–class power hogs. In particular, if the radio receiver is always on in order to listen for incoming email, the battery may drain fairly quickly. On the other hand, if the radio is switched off after, say 1 minute of being idle, incoming messages may be missed, which is clearly undesirable. One efficient solution to this problem has been proposed by Kravets Krishnan. The heart of their solution exploits the fact that mobile computers communicate with fired based stations that have large memories and disk and no power constraints.

CHAPTER 7

PROTECTION AND SECURITY

7.1. Production

The processes in an operating system must be protected from one another's activities. To provide such protection, we can use various mechanisms to ensure that only processes that have gained proper authorization from the operating system can operate on the files, memory segments, CPU, and other resources of a system.

Protection refers to a mechanism for controlling the access of programs, processes, or users to the resources defined by a computer system. This mechanism must provide a means for specifying the controls to be imposed, together with a means of enforcement. We distinguish between protection and security, which is a measure of confidence that the integrity of a system and its data will be preserved.

7.2. Goals of Protection

As computer systems have become more sophisticated and pervasive in their applications, the need to protect their integrity has also grown. Protection was originally conceived as an adjunct to multiprogramming operating systems, so that untrustworthy users might safely share a common logical name space, such as a directory of files, or share a common physical name space, such as memory. Modern protection concepts have evolved to increase the reliability of any complex system that makes use of shared resources.

We need to provide protection for several reasons. The most obvious is the need to prevent the mischievous, intentional violation of an access restriction by a user. Of more general importance, however, is the need to ensure that each program component active in a system uses system resources only in ways consistent with stated policies. This requirement is an absolute one for a reliable system.

Protection can improve reliability by detecting latent errors at the interfaces between component subsystems.

Early detection of interface errors can often prevent contamination of a healthy subsystem by a malfunctioning subsystem. Also, an unprotected resource cannot defend against use (or misuse) by an unauthorized or incompetent user. A protection-oriented system provides means to distinguish between authorized and unauthorized usage.

The role of protection in a computer system is to provide a mechanism for the enforcement of the policies governing resource use. These policies can be established in a variety of ways. Some are fixed in the design of the system, while others are formulated by the management of a system. Still others are defined by the individual users to protect their own files and programs. A protection system must have the flexibility to enforce a variety of policies.

Policies for resource use may vary by application, and they may change over time. For these reasons, protection is no longer the concern solely of the designer of an operating system. The application programmer needs to use protection mechanisms as well, to guard resources created and supported by an application subsystem against misuse. In this chapter, we describe the protection mechanisms the operating system should provide, but application designers can use them as well in designing their own protection software.

Note that mechanisms are distinct from policies. Mechanisms determine how something will be done; policies decide what will be done. The separation of policy and mechanism is important for flexibility. Policies are likely to change from place to place or time to time. In the worst case, every change in policy would require a change in the underlying mechanism. Using general mechanisms enables us to avoid such a situation.

7.3.   Principles of Protection

Frequently, a guiding principle can be used throughout a project, such as the design of an operating system. Following this principle simplifies design decisions and keeps the system consistent and easy to understand. A key, time-tested guiding principle for protection is the principle of least privilege. It dictates that programs, users, and even systems be given just enough privileges to perform their tasks.

Consider the analogy of a security guard with a passkey. If this key allows the guard into just the public areas that she guards, then misuse of the key will result in minimal damage. If, however, the passkey allows access to all areas, then damage from its being lost, stolen, misused, copied, or otherwise compromised will be much greater.

An operating system following the principle of least privilege implements its features, programs, system calls, and data structures so that failure or compromise of a component does the minimum damage and allows the minimum damage to be done. The overflow of a buffer in a system daemon might cause the daemon process to fail, for example, but should not allow the execution of code from the daemon process's stack that would enable a remote user to gain maximum privileges and access to the entire system (as happens too often today).

Such an operating system also provides system calls and services that allow applications to be written with fine-grained access controls. It provides mechanisms to enable privileges when they are needed and to disable them when they are not needed. Also beneficial is the creation of audit trails for all privileged function access. The audit trail allows the programmer, system administrator, or law-enforcement officer to trace all protection and security activities on the system.

Managing users with the principle of least privilege entails creating a separate account for each user, with just the privileges that the user needs. An operator who needs to mount tapes and back up files on the system has access to just those commands and files needed to accomplish the job. Some systems implement role-based access control (RBAC) to provide this functionality.

Computers implemented in a computing facility under the principle of least privilege can be limited to running specific services, accessing specific remote hosts via specific services, and doing so during specific times. Typically, these restrictions are implemented through enabling or disabling each service and through using access control lists.

The principle of least privilege can help produce a more secure computing environment. Unfortunately, it frequently does not. For example, Windows 2000 has a complex protection scheme at its core and yet has many security holes. By comparison, Solaris is considered relatively secure, even though it is a variant of UNIX, which historically was designed with little protection in mind. One reason for the difference may be that Windows 2000 has more lines of code and more services than Solaris and thus has more to secure and protect. Another reason could be that the protection scheme in Windows 2000 is incomplete or protects the wrong aspects of the operating system, leaving other areas vulnerable.

7.4.   Domain of Protection

A computer system is a collection of processes and objects. By objects, we mean both hardware objects (such as the CPU, memory segments, printers, disks, and tape drives) and software objects (such as files, programs, and semaphores). Each object has a unique name that differentiates it from all other objects in the system, and each can be accessed only through well-defined and meaningful operations. Objects are essentially abstract data types.

The operations that are possible may depend on the object. For example, on a CPU, we can only execute. Memory segments can be read and written, whereas a CD-ROM or DVD-ROM can only be read. Tape drives can be read, written, and rewound. Data files can be created, opened, read, written, closed, and deleted; program files can be read, written, executed, and deleted.

A process should be allowed to access only those resources for which it has authorization. Furthermore, at any time, a process should be able to access only those resources that it currently requires to complete its task. This second requirement, commonly referred to as the need-to-know principle, is useful in limiting the amount of damage a faulty process can cause in the system. For example, when process p invokes procedure A(), the procedure should be allowed to access only its own variables and the formal parameters passed to it; it should not be able to access all the variables of process p. Similarly, consider the case in which process p invokes a compiler to compile a particular file. The compiler should not be able to access files arbitrarily but should have access only to a well-defined subset of files (such as the source file, listing file, and so on) related to the file to be compiled. Conversely, the compiler may have private files used for accounting or optimization purposes that process p should not be able to access. The need-to-know principle is similar to the principle of least privilege, in that the goals of protection are to minimize the risks of possible security violations.

Domain Structure

To facilitate the scheme just described, a process operates within a protection domain, which specifies the resources that the process may access. Each domain defines a set of objects and the types of operations that may be invoked on each object. The ability to execute an operation on an object is an access right. A domain is a collection of access rights, each of which is an ordered pair *<object-name, rights-set>*. For example, if domain D has the access right *<file F* , {read, write}>, then a process executing in domain D can both read and write file F. It cannot, however, perform any other operation on that object.

Domains may share access rights. For example, in Figure 7.1, we have three domains: $D_1, D_2,$ and D_3. The access right $<O_4, \{print\}>$ is shared by D_2 and D_3, implying that a process executing in either of these two domains can print object O_4. Note that a process must be executing in domain D_1 to read and write object O_1, while only processes in domain D_3 may execute object O_1.

The association between a process and a domain may be either static, if the set of resources available to the process is fixed throughout the process's lifetime, or dynamic. As might be expected, establishing dynamic protection domains is more complicated than establishing static protection domains.

If the association between processes and domains is fixed, and we want to adhere to the need-to-know principle, then a mechanism must be available to change the content of a domain. The reason stems from the fact that a process may execute in two different phases and may, for example, need read access in one phase and write access in another. If a domain is static, we must define the domain to include both read and write access. However, this arrangement provides more rights than are needed in each of the two phases, since we have read access in the phase where we need only write access, and vice versa. Thus, the need-to-know principle is violated. We must allow the contents of a domain to be modified so that the domain always reflects the minimum necessary access rights.

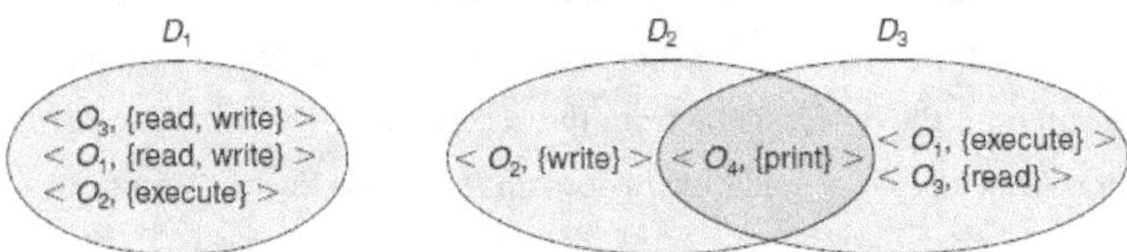

Figure 7.1: System with Three Protection Domains

If the association is dynamic, a mechanism is available to allow domain switching, enabling the process to switch from one domain to another. We may also want to allow the content of a domain to be changed. If we cannot change the content of a domain, we can provide the same effect by creating a new domain with the changed content and switching to that new domain when we want to change the domain content.

A domain can be realized in a variety of ways:

- Each **user** may be a domain. In this case, the set of objects that can be accessed depends on the identity of the user. Domain switching occurs when the user is changed—generally when one user logs out and another user logs in.

- Each **process** may be a domain. In this case, the set of objects that can be accessed depends on the identity of the process. Domain switching occurs when one process sends a message to another process and then waits for a response.

- Each **procedure** may be a domain. In this case, the set of objects that can be accessed corresponds to the local variables defined within the procedure. Domain switching occurs when a procedure call is made.

Consider the standard dual-mode (monitor–user mode) model of operating-system execution. When a process executes in monitor mode, it can execute privileged instructions and thus gain complete control of the computer system. In contrast, when a process executes in user mode, it can invoke only nonprivileged instructions. Consequently, it can execute only within its predefined memory space. These two modes protect the operating system (executing in monitor domain) from the user processes (executing in user domain). In a multiprogrammed operating system, two protection domains are insufficient, since users also want to be protected from one another. Therefore, a more elaborate scheme is needed. We illustrate such a scheme by examining two influential operating systems-UNIX and MULTICS-to see how they implement these concepts.

7.5. Access Matrix

Our general model of protection can be viewed abstractly as a matrix, called an **access matrix**. The rows of the access matrix represent domains, and the columns represent objects. Each entry in the matrix consists of a set of access rights. Because the column defines objects explicitly, we can omit the object name from the access right. The entry access(i,j) defines the set of operations that a process executing in domain D_i can invoke on object O_j.

To illustrate these concepts, we consider the access matrix shown in Figure 7.2. There are four domains and four objects—three files (F_1, F_2, F_3) and one laser printer. A process executing in domain D_1 can read files F_1 and F_3. A process executing in domain D_4 has the same privileges as one executing in domain D_1; but in addition, it can also write onto files F_1 and F_3. The laser printer can be accessed only by a process executing in domain D_2.

object domain	F_1	F_2	F_3	printer
D_1	read		read	
D_2				print
D_3		read	execute	
D_4	read write		read write	

Figure 7.2: Access Matrix

The access-matrix scheme provides us with the mechanism for specifying a variety of policies. The mechanism consists of implementing the access matrix and ensuring that the semantic properties we have outlined hold. More specifically, we must ensure that a process executing in domain D_i can access only those objects specified in row i, and then only as allowed by the access-matrix entries.

The access matrix can implement policy decisions concerning protection. The policy decisions involve which rights should be included in the $(i, j)^{th}$ entry. We must also decide the domain in which each process executes. This last policy is usually decided by the operating system.

The users normally decide the contents of the access-matrix entries. When a user creates a new object O_j, the column O_j is added to the access matrix with the appropriate initialization entries, as dictated by the creator. The user may decide to enter some rights in some entries in column j and other rights in other entries, as needed.

The access matrix provides an appropriate mechanism for defining and implementing strict control for both static and dynamic association between processes and domains. When we switch a process from one domain to another, we are executing an operation (switch) on an object (the domain). We can control domain switching by including domains among the objects of the access matrix.

Similarly, when we change the content of the access matrix, we are performing an operation on an object: the access matrix. Again, we can control these changes by including the access matrix itself as an object. Actually, since each entry in the access matrix can be modified individually, we must consider each entry in the access matrix as an object to be protected. Now, we need to consider only the operations possible on these new objects (domains and the access matrix) and decide how we want processes to be able to execute these operations.

Processes should be able to switch from one domain to another. Switching from domain D_i to domain D_j is allowed if and only if the access right switch $\in access(i, j)$. Thus, in Figure 7.3, a process executing in domain D_2 can switch to domain D_3 or to domain D_4. A process in domain D_4 can switch to D_1, and one in domain D_1 can switch to D_2.

object domain	F_1	F_2	F_3	laser printer	D_1	D_2	D_3	D_4
D_1	read		read			switch		
D_2				print			switch	switch
D_3		read	execute					
D_4	read write		read write		switch			

Figure 7.3: Access Matrix with Domains as Objects

Allowing controlled change in the contents of the access-matrix entries requires three additional operations: copy, owner, and control. We examine these operations next.

The ability to copy an access right from one domain (or row) of the access matrix to another is denoted by an asterisk (*) appended to the access right. The copy right allows the access right to be copied only within the column (that is, for the object) for which the right is defined. For example, in figure 7.4(a), a process executing in domain D_2 can copy the read operation into any entry associated with file F_2. Hence, the access matrix of figure 7.4(a) can be modified to the access matrix shown in figure 7.4(b).

This scheme has two additional variants:

- A right is copied from access(i, j) to access(k, j); it is then removed from access(i, j). This action is a of a right, rather than a copy.
- Propagation of the copy right may be limited. That is, when the right $R*$ is copied from access(i, j) to access(k, j), only the right R (not $R*$) is created. A process executing in domain D_k cannot further copy the right R.

A system may select only one of these three copy rights, or it may provide all three by identifying them as separate rights: copy, transfer, and limited copy.

We also need a mechanism to allow addition of new rights and removal of some rights. The owner right controls these operations. If access(i, j) includes the owner right, then a process executing in domain D_i can add and remove any right in any entry in column j. For example, in figure 7.5(a), domain D_1 is the owner of F_1 and thus can add and delete any valid right in column F_1. Similarly, domain D_2 is the owner of F_2 and F_3 and thus can add and remove any valid right within these two columns. Thus, the access matrix of figure 7.5(a) can be modified to the access matrix shown in figure 7.5(b).

object domain	F_1	F_2	F_3
D_1	owner execute		write
D_2		read* owner	read* owner write
D_3	execute		

(a)

object domain	F_1	F_2	F_3
D_1	owner execute		write
D_2		owner read* write*	read* owner write
D_3		write	write

(b)

Figure 7.4: Access Matrix with Copy Rights

object / domain	F_1	F_2	F_3
D_1	execute		write*
D_2	execute	read*	execute
D_3	execute		

(a)

object / domain	F_1	F_2	F_3
D_1	execute		write*
D_2	execute	read*	execute
D_3	execute	read	

(b)

Figure 7.5: Access Matrix with Owner Rights

The copy and owner rights allow a process to change the entries in a column. A mechanism is also needed to change the entries in a row. The control right is applicable only to domain objects. If access(i, j) includes the control right, then a process executing in domain D_i can remove any access right from row j. For example, suppose that, in Figure 7.3, we include the control right in access(D_2, D_4). Then, a process executing in domain D_2 could modify domain D_4, as shown in Figure 7.6.

The copy and owner rights provide us with a mechanism to limit the propagation of access rights. However, they do not give us the appropriate tools for preventing the propagation (or disclosure) of information. The problem of guaranteeing that no information initially held in an object can migrate outside of its execution environment is called the confinement problem. This problem is in general unsolvable.

These operations on the domains and the access matrix are not in themselves important, but they illustrate the ability of the access-matrix model to allow us to implement and control dynamic protection requirements. New objects and new domains can be created dynamically and included in the access-matrix model. However, we have shown only that the basic mechanism exists. System designers and users must make the policy decisions concerning which domains are to have access to which objects in which ways.

object / domain	F_1	F_2	F_3	laser printer	D_1	D_2	D_3	D_4
D_1	read		read			switch		
D_2				print			switch	switch control
D_3		read	execute					
D_4	write		write		switch			

Figure 7.6: Modified Access Matrix of Figure 7.3

7.6. Implementation of the Access Matrix

How can the access matrix be implemented effectively? In general, the matrix will be sparse; that is, most of the entries will be empty. Although data-structure techniques are available for representing sparse matrices, they are not particularly useful for this application, because of the way in which the protection facility is used. Here, we first describe several methods of implementing the access matrix and then compare the methods.

7.6.1. Global Table

The simplest implementation of the access matrix is a global table consisting of a set of ordered triples <domain, object, rights-set>. Whenever an operation M is executed on an object O_j within domain D_i, the global table is searched for a triple $<D_i, O_j, R_k>$, with $M \in R_k$. If this triple is found, the operation is allowed to continue; otherwise, an exception (or error) condition is raised.

This implementation suffers from several drawbacks. The table is usually large and thus cannot be kept in main memory, so additional I/O is needed. Virtual memory techniques are often used for managing this table. In addition, it is difficult to take advantage of special groupings of objects or domains. For example, if everyone can read a particular object, this object must have a separate entry in every domain.

7.6.2. Access Lists for Objects

Each column in the access matrix can be implemented as an access list for one object. Obviously, the empty entries can be discarded. The resulting list for each object consists of ordered pairs <domain, rights-set>, which define all domains with a nonempty set of access rights for that object.

This approach can be extended easily to define a list plus a ***default*** set of access rights. When an operation M on an object O_j is attempted in domain D_i, we search the access list for object O_j, looking for an entry <D_i, R_k> with $M \in R_k$. If the entry is found, we allow the operation; if it is not, we check the default set. If M is in the default set, we allow the access. Otherwise, access is denied, and an exception condition occurs. For efficiency, we may check the default set first and then search the access list.

7.6.3. Capability Lists for Domains

Rather than associating the columns of the access matrix with the objects as access lists, we can associate each row with its domain. A **capability list** for a domain is a list of objects together with the operations allowed on those objects. An object is often represented by its physical name or address, called a **capability**. To execute operation M on object O_j, the process executes the operation M, specifying the capability (or pointer) for object O_j as a parameter. Simple possession of the capability means that access is allowed.

The capability list is associated with a domain, but it is never directly accessible to a process executing in that domain. Rather, the capability list is itself a protected object, maintained by the operating system and accessed by the user only indirectly. Capability-based protection relies on the fact that the capabilities are never allowed to migrate into any address space directly accessible by a user process (where they could be modified). If all capabilities are secure, the object they protect is also secure against unauthorized access.

Capabilities were originally proposed as a kind of secure pointer, to meet the need for resource protection that was foreseen as multiprogrammed computer systems came of age. The idea of an inherently protected pointer provides a foundation for protection that can be extended up to the application level.

To provide inherent protection, we must distinguish capabilities from other kinds of objects, and they must be interpreted by an abstract machine on which higher-level programs run. Capabilities are usually distinguished from other data in one of two ways:

- Each object has a **tag** to denote whether it is a capability or accessible data. The tags themselves must not be directly accessible by an application program. Hardware or firmware support may be used to enforce this restriction. Although only one bit is necessary to distinguish between capabilities and other objects, more bits are often used. This extension allows all objects to be tagged with their types by the hardware. Thus, the hardware can distinguish integers, floating-point numbers, pointers, Booleans, characters, instructions, capabilities, and uninitialized values by their tags.

- Alternatively, the address space associated with a program can be split into two parts. One part is accessible to the program and contains the program's normal data and instructions. The other part, containing the capability list, is accessible only by the operating system. A segmented memory space is useful to support this approach.

Several capability-based protection systems have been developed. The Mach operating system also uses a version of capability-based protection.

7.6.4. A Lock–Key Mechanism

The **lock–key scheme** is a compromise between access lists and capability lists. Each object has a list of unique bit patterns, called **locks**. Similarly, each domain has a list of unique bit patterns, called **keys**. A process executing in a domain can access an object only if that domain has a key that matches one of the locks of the object.

As with capability lists, the list of keys for a domain must be managed by the operating system on behalf of the domain. Users are not allowed to examine or modify the list of keys (or locks) directly.

7.6.5. Comparison

As you might expect, choosing a technique for implementing an access matrix involves various trade-offs. Using a global table is simple; however, the table can be quite large and often cannot take advantage of special groupings of objects or domains. Access lists correspond directly to the needs of users. When a user creates an object, he can specify which domains can access the object, as well as what operations are allowed. However, because access-right information for a particular domain is not localized, determining the set of access rights for each domain is difficult. In addition, every access to the object must be checked, requiring a search of the access list. In a large system with long access lists, this search can be time consuming.

Capability lists do not correspond directly to the needs of users, but they are useful for localizing information for a given process. The process attempting access must present a capability for that access. Then, the protection system needs only to verify that the capability is valid. Revocation of capabilities, however, may be inefficient.

The lock–key mechanism, as mentioned, is a compromise between access lists and capability lists. The mechanism can be both effective and flexible, depending on the length of the keys. The keys can be passed freely from domain to domain. In addition, access privileges can be effectively revoked by the simple technique of changing some of the locks associated with the object.

Most systems use a combination of access lists and capabilities. When a process first tries to access an object, the access list is searched. If access is denied, an exception condition occurs. Otherwise, a capability is created and attached to the process. Additional references use the capability to demonstrate swiftly that access is allowed. After the last access, the capability is destroyed. This strategy is used in the MULTICS system and in the CAL system.

As an example of how such a strategy works, consider a file system in which each file has an associated access list. When a process opens a file, the directory structure is searched to find the file, access permission is checked, and buffers are allocated. All this information is recorded in a new entry in a file table associated with the process. The operation returns an index into this table for the newly opened file. All operations on the file are made by specification of the index into the file table. The entry in the file table then points to the file and its buffers. When the file is closed, the file-table entry is deleted. Since the file table is maintained by the operating system, the user cannot accidentally corrupt it. Thus, the user can access only those files that have been opened. Since access is checked when the file is opened, protection is ensured. This strategy is used in the UNIX system.

The right to access must still be checked on each access, and the file-table entry has a capability only for the allowed operations. If a file is opened for reading, then a capability for read access is placed in the file-table entry. If an attempt is made to write onto the file, the system identifies this protection violation by comparing the requested operation with the capability in the file-table entry.

7.7. Access Control

Access controls can be used on files within a file system. Each file and directory is assigned an owner, a group, or possibly a list of users, and for each of those entities, access-control information is assigned. A similar function can be added to other aspects of a computer system. A good example of this is found in Solaris 10.

Solaris 10 advances the protection available in the operating system by explicitly adding the principle of least privilege via **role-based access control (RBAC)**. This facility revolves around privileges. A privilege is the right to execute a system call or to use an option within that system call (such as opening a file with write access). Privileges can be assigned to processes, limiting them to exactly the access they need to perform their work. Privileges and programs can also be assigned to **roles**. Users are assigned roles or can take roles based on passwords to the roles. In this way, a user can take a role that enables a privilege, allowing the user to run a program to accomplish a specific task, as depicted figure 7.7. This implementation of privileges decreases the security risk associated with super users and setuid programs.

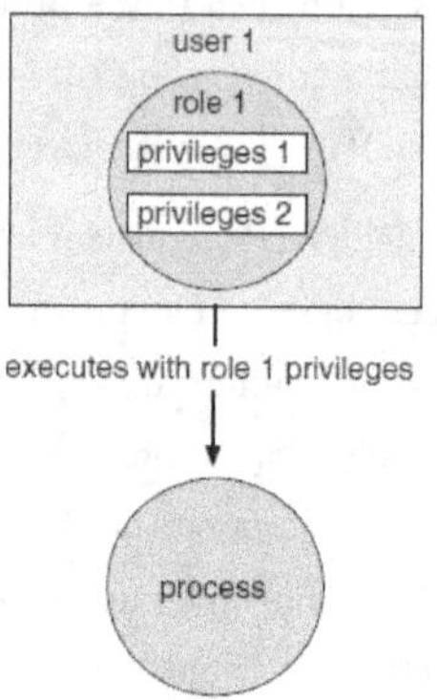

Figure 7.7: Role-based Access Control in Solaris 10

7.8.   Revocation of Access Rights

In a dynamic protection system, we may sometimes need to revoke access rights to objects shared by different users. Various questions about revocation may arise:

- **Immediate versus delayed**: Does revocation occur immediately, or is it delayed? If revocation is delayed, can we find out when it will take place?

- **Selective versus general**: When an access right to an object is revoked, does it affect all the users who have an access right to that object, or can we specify a select group of users whose access rights should be revoked?

- **Partial versus total**: Can a subset of the rights associated with an object be revoked, or must we revoke all access rights for this object?

- **Temporary versus permanent**: Can access be revoked permanently (that is, the revoked access right will never again be available), or can access be revoked and later be obtained again?

With an access-list scheme, revocation is easy. The access list is searched for any access rights to be revoked, and they are deleted from the list. Revocation is immediate and can be general or selective, total or partial, and permanent or temporary.

Capabilities, however, present a much more difficult revocation problem, as mentioned earlier. Since the capabilities are distributed throughout the system, we must find them before we can revoke them.

Schemes that implement revocation for capabilities include the following:

- **Reacquisition**: Periodically, capabilities are deleted from each domain. If a process wants to use a capability, it may find that that capability has been deleted. The process may then try to reacquire the capability. If access has been revoked, the process will not be able to reacquire the capability.

- **Back-pointers**: A list of pointers is maintained with each object, pointing to all capabilities associated with that object. When revocation is required, we can follow these pointers, changing the capabilities as necessary. This scheme was adopted in the MULTICS system. It is quite general, but its implementation is costly.

- **Indirection**: The capabilities point indirectly, not directly, to the objects. Each capability points to a unique entry in a global table, which in turn points to the object. We implement revocation by searching the global table for the desired entry and deleting it. Then, when an access is attempted, the capability is found to point to an illegal table entry. Table entries can be reused for other capabilities without difficulty, since both the capability and the table entry contain the unique name of the object. The object for a capability and its table entry must match. This scheme was adopted in the CAL system. It does not allow selective revocation.

- **Keys**: A key is a unique bit pattern that can be associated with a capability. This key is defined when the capability is created, and it can be neither modified nor inspected by the process that owns the capability. A **master key** is associated with each object; it can be defined or replaced with the set-key operation. When a capability is created, the current value of the master key is associated with the capability. When the capability is exercised, its key is compared with the master key. If the keys match, the operation is allowed to continue; otherwise, an exception condition is raised. Revocation replaces the master key with a new value via the set-key operation, invalidating all previous capabilities for this object.

This scheme does not allow selective revocation, since only one master key is associated with each object. If we associate a list of keys with each object, then selective revocation can be implemented. Finally, we can group all keys into one global table of keys. A capability is valid only if its key matches some key in the global table. We implement revocation by removing the matching key from the table. With this scheme, a key can be associated with several objects, and several keys can be associated with each object, providing maximum flexibility.

In key-based schemes, the operations of defining keys, inserting them into lists, and deleting them from lists should not be available to all users. In particular, it would be reasonable to allow only the owner of an object to set the keys for that object. This choice, however, is a policy decision that the protection system can implement but should not define.

7.9. Capability-Based Systems

In this section, we survey two capability-based protection systems. These systems differ in their complexity and in the types of policies that can be implemented on them. Neither system is widely used, but both provide interesting proving grounds for protection theories.

7.9.1. AN Example: HYDRA

Hydra is a capability-based protection system that provides considerable flexibility. The system implements a fixed set of possible access rights, including such basic forms of access as the right to read, write, or execute a memory segment. In addition, a user (of the protection system) can declare other rights. The interpretation of user-defined rights is performed solely by the user's program, but the system provides access protection for the use of these rights, as well as for the use of system-defined rights. These facilities constitute a significant development in protection technology.

Operations on objects are defined procedurally. The procedures that implement such operations are themselves a form of object, and they are accessed indirectly by capabilities. The names of user-defined procedures must be identified to the protection system if it is to deal with objects of the user-defined type. When the definition of an object is made known to Hydra, the names of operations on the type become **auxiliary rights**.

Auxiliary rights can be described in a capability for an instance of the type. For a process to perform an operation on a typed object, the capability it holds for that object must contain the name of the operation being invoked among its auxiliary rights. This restriction enables discrimination of access rights to be made on an instance-by-instance and process-by-process basis.

Hydra also provides **rights amplification**. This scheme allows a procedure to be certified as *trustworthy* to act on a formal parameter of a specified type on behalf of any process that holds a right to execute the procedure. The rights held by a trustworthy procedure are independent of, and may exceed, the rights held by the calling process. However, such a procedure must not be regarded as universally trustworthy (the procedure is not allowed to act on other types, for instance), and the trustworthiness must not be extended to any other procedures or program segments that might be executed by a process.

Amplification allows implementation procedures access to the representation variables of an abstract data type. If a process holds a capability to a typed object A, for instance, this capability may include an auxiliary right to invoke some operation P but does not include any of the so-called kernel rights, such as read, write, or execute, on the segment that represents A. Such a capability gives a process a means of indirect access (through the operation P) to the representation of A, but only for specific purposes.

When a process invokes the operation P on an object A, however, the capability for access to A may be amplified as control passes to the code body of P. This amplification may be necessary to allow P the right to access the storage segment representing A so as to implement the operation that P defines on the abstract data type. The code body of P may be allowed to read or to write to the segment of A directly, even though the calling process cannot. On return from P, the capability for A is restored to its original, unamplified state. This case is a typical one in which the rights held by a process for access to a protected segment must change dynamically, depending on the task to be performed. The dynamic adjustment of rights is performed to guarantee consistency of a programmer-defined abstraction. Amplification of rights can be stated explicitly in the declaration of an abstract type to the Hydra operating system.

When a user passes an object as an argument to a procedure, we may need to ensure that the procedure cannot modify the object. We can implement this restriction readily by passing an access right that does not have the modification (write) right. However, if amplification may occur, the right to modify may be reinstated. Thus, the user-protection requirement can be circumvented. In general, of course, a user may trust that a procedure performs its task correctly. This assumption is not always correct, however, because of hardware or software errors. Hydra solves this problem by restricting amplifications.

The procedure-call mechanism of Hydra was designed as a direct solution to the **problem of mutually suspicious subsystems**. This problem is defined as follows. Suppose that a program can be invoked as a service by a number of different users (for example, a sort routine, a compiler, a game). When users invoke this service program, they take the risk that the program will malfunction and will either damage the given data or retain some access right to the data to be used (without authority) later. Similarly, the service program may have some private files (for accounting purposes, for example) that should not be accessed directly by the calling user program. Hydra provides mechanisms for directly dealing with this problem.

A Hydra subsystem is built on top of its protection kernel and may require protection of its own components. A subsystem interacts with the kernel through calls on a set of kernel-defined primitives that define access rights to resources defined by the subsystem. The subsystem designer can define policies for use of these resources by user processes, but the policies are enforced by use of the standard access protection provided by the capability system.

Programmers can make direct use of the protection system after acquainting themselves with its features in the appropriate reference manual. Hydra provides a large library of system-defined procedures that can be called by user programs. Programmers can explicitly incorporate calls on these system procedures into their program code or can use a program translator that has been interfaced to Hydra.

7.9.2. *AN Example: Cambridge CAP System*

A different approach to capability-based protection has been taken in the design of the Cambridge CAP system. CAP's capability system is simpler and superficially less powerful than that of Hydra. However, closer examination shows that it, too, can be used to provide secure protection of user-defined objects. CAP has two kinds of capabilities. The ordinary kind is called a **data capability**. It can be used to provide access to objects, but the only rights provided are the standard read, write, and execute of the individual storage segments associated with the object. Data capabilities are interpreted by microcode in the CAP machine.

The second kind of capability is the so-called **software capability**, which is protected, but not interpreted, by the CAP microcode. It is interpreted by a *protected* (that is, privileged) procedure, which may be written by an application programmer as part of a subsystem. A particular kind of rights amplification is associated with a protected procedure. When executing the code body of such a procedure, a process temporarily acquires the right to read or write the contents of a software capability itself. This specific kind of rights amplification corresponds to an implementation of the seal and unseals primitives on capabilities. Of course, this privilege is still subject to type verification to ensure that only software capabilities for a specified abstract type are passed to any such procedure. Universal trust is not placed in any code other than the CAP machine's microcode. (See the bibliographical notes at the end of the chapter for references.)

The interpretation of a software capability is left completely to the subsystem, through the protected procedures it contains. This scheme allows a variety of protection policies to be implemented. Although programmers can define their own protected procedures (any of which might be incorrect), the security of the overall system cannot be compromised. The basic protection system will not allow an unverified, user-defined, protected procedure access to any storage segments (or capabilities) that do not belong to the protection environment in which it resides. The most serious consequence of an insecure protected procedure is a protection breakdown of the subsystem for which that procedure has responsibility.

The designers of the CAP system have noted that the use of software capabilities allowed them to realize considerable economies in formulating and implementing protection policies commensurate with the requirements of abstract resources. However, subsystem designers who want to make use of this facility cannot simply study a reference manual, as is the case with Hydra. Instead, they must learn the principles and techniques of protection, since the system provides them with no library of procedures.

7.10. Language-Based Protection

To the degree that protection is provided in existing computer systems, it is usually achieved through an operating-system kernel, which acts as a security agent to inspect and validate each attempt to access a protected resource. Since comprehensive access validation may be a source of considerable overhead, either we must give it hardware support to reduce the cost of each validation, or we must allow the system designer to compromise the goals of protection. Satisfying all these goals is difficult if the flexibility to implement protection policies is restricted by the support mechanisms provided or if protection environments are made larger than necessary to secure greater operational efficiency.

As operating systems have become more complex, and particularly as they have attempted to provide higher-level user interfaces, the goals of protection have become much more refined. The designers of protection systems have drawn heavily on ideas that originated in programming languages and especially on the concepts of abstract data types and objects. Protection systems are now concerned not only with the identity of a resource to which access is attempted but also with the functional nature of that access. In the newest protection systems, concern for the function to be invoked extends beyond a set of system-defined functions, such as standard file-access methods, to include functions that may be user-defined as well.

Policies for resource use may also vary, depending on the application, and they may be subject to change over time. For these reasons, protection can no longer be considered a matter of concern only to the designer of an operating system. It should also be available as a tool for use by the application designer, so that resources of an application subsystem can be guarded against tampering or the influence of an error.

7.10.1. Compiler-based Enforcement

At this point, programming languages enter the picture. Specifying the desired control of access to a shared resource in a system is making a declarative statement about the resource. This kind of statement can be integrated into a language by an extension of its typing facility. When protection is declared along with data typing, the designer of each subsystem can specify its requirements for protection, as well as its need for use of other resources in a system. Such a specification should be given directly as a program is composed, and in the language in which the program itself is stated. This approach has several significant advantages:

- Protection needs are simply declared, rather than programmed as a sequence of calls on procedures of an operating system.
- Protection requirements can be stated independently of the facilities provided by a particular operating system.
- The means for enforcement need not be provided by the designer of a subsystem.
- A declarative notation is natural because access privileges are closely related to the linguistic concept of data type.

A variety of techniques can be provided by a programming-language implementation to enforce protection, but any of these must depend on some degree of support from an underlying machine and its operating system. For example, suppose a language is used to generate code to run on the Cambridge CAP system. On this system, every storage reference made on the underlying hardware occurs indirectly through a capability. This restriction prevents any process from accessing a resource outside of its protection environment at any time. However, a program may impose arbitrary restrictions on how a resource can be used during execution of a particular code segment. We can implement such restrictions most readily by using the software capabilities provided by CAP. A language implementation might provide standard protected procedures to interpret software capabilities that would realize the protection policies that could be specified in the language. This scheme puts policy specification at the disposal of the programmers, while freeing them from implementing its enforcement.

Even if a system does not provide a protection kernel as powerful as those of Hydra or CAP, mechanisms are still available for implementing protection specifications given in a programming language. The principal distinction is that the *security* of this protection will not be as great as that supported by a protection kernel, because the mechanism must rely on more assumptions about the operational state of the system. A compiler can separate references for which it can certify that no protection violation could occur from those for which a violation might be possible, and it can treat them differently. The security provided by this form of protection rests on the assumption that the code generated by the compiler will not be modified prior to or during its execution.

What, then, are the relative merits of enforcement based solely on a kernel, as opposed to enforcement provided largely by a compiler?

- **Security**: Enforcement by a kernel provides a greater degree of security of the protection system itself than does the generation of protection-checking code by a compiler. In a compiler-supported scheme, security rests on correctness of the translator, on some underlying mechanism of storage management that protects the segments from which compiled code is executed, and, ultimately, on the security of files from which a program is loaded. Some of these considerations also apply to a software-supported protection kernel, but to a lesser degree, since the kernel may reside in fixed physical storage segments and may be loaded only from a designated file. With a tagged-capability system, in which all address computation is performed either by hardware or by a fixed microprogram, even greater security is possible. Hardware-supported protection is also relatively immune to protection violations that might occur as a result of either hardware or system software malfunction.

- **Flexibility**: There are limits to the flexibility of a protection kernel in implementing a user-defined policy, although it may supply adequate facilities for the system to provide enforcement of its own policies. With a programming language, protection policy can be declared and enforcement provided as needed by an implementation. If a language does not provide sufficient flexibility, it can be extended or replaced with less disturbance than would be caused by the modification of an operating-system kernel.

- **Efficiency**: The greatest efficiency is obtained when enforcement of protection is supported directly by hardware (or microcode). Insofar as software support is required, language-based enforcement has the advantage that static access enforcement can be verified off-line at compile time. Also, since an intelligent compiler can tailor the enforcement mechanism to meet the specified need, the fixed overhead of kernel calls can often be avoided.

In summary, the specification of protection in a programming language allows the high-level description of policies for the allocation and use of resources. A language implementation can provide software for protection enforcement when automatic hardware-supported checking is unavailable. In addition, it can interpret protection specifications to generate calls on whatever protection system is provided by the hardware and the operating system.

One way of making protection available to the application program is through the use of a software capability that could be used as an object of computation. Inherent in this concept is the idea that certain program components might have the privilege of creating or examining these software capabilities. A capability-creating program would be able to execute a primitive operation that would seal a data structure, rendering the latter's contents inaccessible to any program components that did not hold either the seal or the unseal privilege. Such components might copy the data structure or pass its address to other program components, but they could not gain access to its contents. The reason for introducing such software capabilities is to bring a protection mechanism into the programming language. The only problem with the concept as proposed is that the use of the seal and unseal operations takes a procedural approach to specifying protection. A nonprocedural or declarative notation seems a preferable way to make protection available to the application programmer.

What is needed is a safe, dynamic access-control mechanism for distributing capabilities to system resources among user processes. To contribute to the overall reliability of a system, the access-control mechanism should be safe to use. To be useful in practice, it should also be reasonably efficient. This requirement has led to the development of a number of language constructs that allow the programmer to declare various restrictions on the use of a specific managed resource. (See the bibliographical notes for appropriate references). These constructs provide mechanisms for three functions:

- Distributing capabilities safely and efficiently among customer processes. In particular, mechanisms ensure that a user process will use the managed resource only if it was granted a capability to that resource.

- Specifying the type of operations that a particular process may invoke on an allocated resource (for example, a reader of a file should be allowed only to read the file, whereas a writer should be able both to read and to write). It should not be necessary to grant the same set of rights to every user process, and it should be impossible for a process to enlarge its set of access rights, except with the authorization of the access-control mechanism.

- Specifying the order in which a particular process may invoke the various operations of a resource (for example, a file must be opened before it can be read). It should be possible to give two processes different restrictions on the order in which they can invoke the operations of the allocated resource.

The incorporation of protection concepts into programming languages, as a practical tool for system design, is in its infancy. Protection will likely become a matter of greater concern to the designers of new systems with distributed architectures and increasingly stringent requirements on data security. Then the importance of suitable language notations in which to express protection requirements will be recognized more widely.

7.10.2. Protection in JAVA

Because Java was designed to run in a distributed environment, the Java virtual machine-or JVM-has many built-in protection mechanisms. Java programs are composed of **classes**, each of which is a collection of data fields and functions (called **methods**) that operate on those fields. The JVM loads a class in response to a request to create instances (or objects) of that class. One of the most novel and useful features of Java is its support for dynamically loading untrusted classes over a network and for executing mutually distrusting classes within the same JVM.

Because of these capabilities, protection is a paramount concern. Classes running in the same JVM may be from different sources and may not be equally trusted. As a result, enforcing protection at the granularity of the JVM process is insufficient. Intuitively, whether a request to open a file should be allowed will generally depend on which class has requested the open. The operating system lacks this knowledge.

Thus, such protection decisions are handled within the JVM. When the JVM loads a class, it assigns the class to a protection domain that gives the permissions of that class. The protection domain to which the class is assigned depends on the URL from which the class was loaded and any digital signatures on the class file. A configurable policy file determines the permissions granted to the domain (and its classes). For example, classes loaded from a trusted server might be placed in a protection domain that allows them to access files in the user's home directory, whereas classes loaded from an untrusted server might have no file access permissions at all.

It can be complicated for the JVM to determine what class is responsible for a request to access a protected resource. Accesses are often performed indirectly, through system libraries or other classes. For example, consider a class that is not allowed to open network connections. It could call a system library to request the load of the contents of a URL. The JVM must decide whether or not to open a network connection for this request. But which class should be used to determine if the connection should be allowed, the application or the system library?

The philosophy adopted in Java is to require the library class to explicitly permit a network connection. More generally, in order to access a protected resource, some method in the calling sequence that resulted in the request must explicitly assert the privilege to access the resource. By doing so, this method *takes responsibility* for the request. Presumably, it will also perform whatever checks are necessary to ensure the safety of the request. Of course, not every method is allowed to assert a privilege; a method can assert a privilege only if its class is in a protection domain that is itself allowed to exercise the privilege.

This implementation approach is called **stack inspection**. Every thread in the JVM has an associated stack of its ongoing method invocations. When a caller may not be trusted, a method executes an access request within a doPrivileged block to perform the access to a protected resource directly or indirectly. doPrivileged() is a static method in the AccessController class that is passed a class with a run() method to invoke. When the doPrivileged block is entered, the stack frame for this method is annotated to indicate this fact. Then, the contents of the block are executed. When an access to a protected resource is subsequently requested, either by this method or a method it calls, a call to checkPermissions() is used to invoke stack inspection to determine if the request should be allowed. The inspection examines stack frames on the calling thread's stack, starting from the most recently added frame and working toward the oldest. If a stack frame is first found that has the doPrivileged()annotation, then checkPermissions() returns immediately and silently, allowing the access. If a stack frame is first found for which access is disallowed based on the protection domain of the method's class, then checkPermissions() throws an AccessControlException. If the stack inspection exhausts the stack without finding either type of frame, then whether access is allowed depends on the implementation (for example, some implementations of the JVM may allow access, while other implementations may not).

Stack inspection is illustrated in Figure 7.8. Here, the gui() method of a class in the *untrusted applet* protection domain performs two operations, first a get() and then an open(). The former is an invocation of the get() method of a class in the *URL loader* protection domain, which is permitted to open() sessions to sites in the lucent.com domain, in particular a proxy serverproxy.lucent.com for retrieving URLs. For this reason, the untrusted applet's get() invocation will succeed: the checkPermissions()call in the networking library encounters the stack frame of the get() method, which performed its open() in a doPrivileged block. However, the untrusted applet's open() invocation will result in an exception, because the checkPermissions() call finds nodoPrivileged annotation before encountering the stack frame of the gui() method.

protection domain:	untrusted applet	URL loader	networking
socket permission:	none	*.lucent.com:80, connect	any

class:	gui:
	 . . .
	   get(url);
	   open(addr);
	 . . .
		get(URL u):
		 . . .
		   doPrivileged {
		     open('proxy.lucent.com:80');
		   }
		   <request u from proxy>
		   . . .
			open(Addr a):
			 . . .
			   checkPermission
			   (a, connect);
			   connect (a);
			   . . .

Figure 7.8: Stack Inspection

Of course, for stack inspection to work, a program must be unable to modify the annotations on its own stack frame or to otherwise manipulate stack inspection. This is one of the most important differences between Java and many other languages (including C++). A Java program cannot directly access memory; it can manipulate only an object for which it has a reference. References cannot be forged, and manipulations are made only through well-defined interfaces. Compliance is enforced through a sophisticated collection of load time and run-time checks. As a result, an object cannot manipulate its runtime stack, because it cannot get a reference to the stack or other components of the protection system.

More generally, Java's load-time and run-time checks enforce **type safety** of Java classes. Type safety ensures that classes cannot treat integers as pointers, write past the end of an array, or otherwise access memory in arbitrary ways. Rather, a program can access an object only via the methods defined on that object by its class. This is the foundation of Java protection, since it enables a class to effectively **encapsulate** and protect its data and methods from other classes loaded in the same JVM. For example, a variable can be defined as private so that only the class that contains it can access it or protected so that it can be accessed only by the class that contains it, subclasses of that class, or classes in the same package. Type safety ensures that these restrictions can be enforced.

7.11. Summary

Computer systems contain many objects, and they need to be protected from misuse. Objects may be hardware (such as memory, CPU time, and I/O devices) or software (such as files, programs, and semaphores). An access right is permission to perform an operation on an object. A domain is a set of access rights. Processes execute in domains and may use any of the access rights in the domain to access and manipulate objects. During its lifetime, a process may be either bound to a protection domain or allowed to switch from one domain to another.

The access matrix is a general model of protection that provides a mechanism for protection without imposing a particular protection policy on the system or its users. The separation of policy and mechanism is an important design property.

The access matrix is sparse. It is normally implemented either as access lists associated with each object or as capability lists associated with each domain. We can include dynamic protection in the access-matrix model by considering domains and the access matrix itself as objects. Revocation of access rights in a dynamic protection model is typically easier to implement with an access-list scheme than with a capability list.

Real systems are much more limited than the general model and tend to provide protection only for files. UNIX is representative, providing read, write, and execution protection separately for the owner, group, and general public for each file.

MULTICS uses a ring structure in addition to file access. Hydra, the Cambridge CAP system, and Mach are capability systems that extend protection to user-defined software objects. Solaris 10 implements the principle of least privilege via role-based access control, a form of the access matrix.

Language-based protection provides finer-grained arbitration of requests and privileges than the operating system is able to provide. For example, a single Java JVM can run several threads, each in a different protection class. It enforces the resource requests through sophisticated stack inspection and via the type safety of the language.

7.12. Security

Many companies possess valuable information they want to guard closely. This information can be technical (e.g., a new chip design or software), commercial (e.g., studies of the competition or marketing plans), financial (e.g., plans for a stock offering) legal (e.g., documents about a potential merger or takeover), among many other possibilities. Frequently this information is protected by having a uniformed guard at the building entrance who checks to see that everyone entering the building is wearing a proper badge. In addition, many offices may be locked and some file cabinets may be locked as well to ensure that only authorized people have access to the information. Home computers increasingly have valuable data on them, too. Many people keep their financial information, including tax returns and credit card numbers, on their computer. Love letters have gone digital. And hard disks these days are full of important photos, videos, and movies.

7.13. The Security Environment

Let us start our study of security by defining some terminology. Some people use the terms "security" and "protection" interchangeably. Nevertheless, it is frequently useful to make a distinction between the general problems involved in making sure that files are not read or modified by unauthorized persons, which include technical, administrative, legal, and political issues on the one hand, and the specific operating system mechanisms used to provide security, on the other. To avoid confusion, we will use the term security to refer to the overall problem, and the term protection mechanisms to refer to the specific operating system mechanisms used to safeguard information in the computer. The boundary between them is not well defined, however. First we will look at security to see what the nature of the problem is. Later on in the chapter we will look at the protection mechanisms and models available to help achieve security. Security has many facets. Three of the more important ones are the nature of the threats, the nature of intruders, and accidental data loss. We will now look at these in turn.

Threats

A threat, in the context of computer security, refers to anything that has the potential to cause serious harm to a computer system. A threat is something that may or may not happen, but has the potential to cause serious damage. Threats can lead to attacks on computer systems, networks and more.

Intruders

Most people are pretty nice and obey the law, so why worry about security? Because there are unfortunately a few people around who are not so nice and want to cause trouble (possibly for their own commercial gain). In the security literature, people who are nosing around places where they have no business being are called intruders or sometimes adversaries. Intruders act in two different ways. Passive intruders just want to read files they are not authorized to read. Active intruders are more malicious; they want to make unauthorized changes to data. When designing a system to be secure against intruders, it is important to keep in mind the kind of intruder one is trying to protect against.

Accidental Data Loss

In addition to threats caused by malicious intruders, valuable data can be lost by accident. Some of the common causes of accidental data loss are:

- **Acts of God:** fires, floods, earthquakes, wars, riots, or rats gnawing backup tapes.
- **Hardware or software errors:** CPU malfunctions, unreadable disks or tapes, telecommunication errors, program bugs.

- **Human errors:** incorrect data entry, wrong tape or CD-ROM mounted, wrong program run, lost disk or tape, or some other mistake.

Most of these can be dealt with by maintaining adequate backups, preferably far away from the original data. While protecting data against accidental loss may seem mundane compared to protecting against clever intruders, in practice, probably more damage is caused by the former than the latter.

7.14. Levels of Security Measures

To protect a system, we must take security measures at four levels:"

- **Physical:** The site or sites containing the computer systems must be physically secured against armed or surreptitious entry by intruders. Both the machine rooms and the terminals or workstations that have access to the machines must be secured.

- **Human:** Authorizing users must be done carefully to assure that only appropriate users have access to the system. Even authorized users, however, may be "encouraged" to let others use their access (in exchange for a bribe, for example). They may also be tricked into allowing access via social engineering. One type of social-engineering attack is phishing. Here, a legitimate-looking e-mail or web page misleads a user into entering confidential information. Another technique is dumpster diving, a general term for attempting to gather information in order to gain unauthorized access to the computer (by looking through trash, finding phone books, or finding notes containing passwords, for example). These security problems are management and personnel issues, not problems pertaining to operating systems.

- **Operating system:** The system must protect itself from accidental or purposeful security breaches. A runaway process could constitute an accidental denial-of-service attack. A query to a service could reveal passwords. A stack overflow could allow the launching of an unauthorized process. The list of possible breaches is almost endless.

- **Network:** Much computer data in modern systems travels over private leased lines, shared lines like the Internet, wireless connections, or dial-up lines. Intercepting these data could be just as harmful as breaking into a computer; and interruption of communications could constitute a remote denial-of-service attack, diminishing users' use of and trust in the system.

Security at the first two levels must be maintained if operating-system security is to be ensured. A weakness at a high level of security (physical or human) allows circumvention of strict low-level (operating-system) security measures. Thus, the old adage that a chain is as weak as its weakest link is especially true of system security. All of these aspects must be addressed for security to be maintained.

7.15. Malware

In ancient times (say, before 2000), bored (but clever) teenagers would sometimes fill their idle hours by writing malicious software that they would then release into the world for the heck of it. This software, which, included Trojan horses, viruses, and worms and collectively called malware often quickly spread around the world. As reports were published about how many millions of dollars of damage the malware caused and how many people lost their valuable data as a result, the authors would be very impressed with their programming skills. To them it was just a fun prank; they were not making any money off it, after all.

Those days are gone. Malware is now written on demand by well-organized criminals who prefer not to see their work publicized in the newspapers. They are in it entirely for the money. A large fraction of all malware is now designed to spread as quickly as possible over the Internet and infect as many machines as it can. When a machine is infected, software is installed that reports the address of the captured machine back to certain machines, often in countries with poorly developed or corrupt judicial systems, for example in some of the former Soviet republics. A backdoor is also installed on the machine that allows the criminals who sent out the malware to easily command the machine to do what it is instructed to do. A machine taken over in this fashion is called a zombie, and a collection of them is called a botnet, a contraction of "robot network."

A criminal who controls a botnet can rent it out for various nefarious (and always commercial) purposes. A common one is for sending out commercial spam. If a major spam attack occurs and the police try to track down the origin, all they see is that it is coming from thousands of machines all over the world. If they approach some of the owners of these machines, they will discover kids, small business owners, housewives, grandmothers, and many other people, all of whom vigorously deny that they are mass spammers. Using other people's machines to do the dirty work, makes it hard to track down the criminals behind the operation.

7.16. Defenses

With problems lurking everywhere, is there any hope of making systems secure? Actually, there is, and in the following sections we will look at some of the ways systems can be designed and implemented to increase their security. One of the most important concepts is defense in depth. Basically, the idea here is that you should have multiple layers of security so that if one of them is breached, there are still others to overcome. Think about a house with a high, spiky, locked iron fence around it, motion detectors in the yard, two industrial-strength locks on the front door, and a computerized burglar alarm system inside. While each technique is valuable by itself, to rob the house the burglar would have to defeat all of them. Properly secured computer systems are like this house, with multiple layers of security. We will now look at some of the layers. The defenses are not really hierarchical, but we will start roughly with the more general outer ones and work our way to more specific ones.

Firewalls

Mechanisms are needed to keep "good" bits in and "bad" bits out. One approach is to use a firewall, which is just a modern adaptation of that old medieval security standby: digging a deep moat around your castle. This design forced everyone entering or leaving the castle to pass over a single drawbridge, where they could be inspected by the I/O police. With networks, the same trick is possible: a company can have many LANs connected in arbitrary ways, but all traffic to or from the company is forced through an electronic drawbridge, the firewall.

Antivirus

Firewalls try to keep intruders out of the computer, but they can fail in various ways, as described above. In that case, the next line of defense comprises the antimalware programs, often called antivirus programs, although many of them also combat worms and spyware. Viruses try to hide and users try to find them, which leads to a cat-and-mouse game. In this respect, viruses are like rootkits, except that most virus writers emphasize rapid spread of the virus rather than playing hide-and-seek as rootkits do.

Jailing

An old Russian saying is: "Trust but Verify." Clearly, the old Russian clearly had software in mind. Even though a piece of software has been signed, a good attitude is to verify that it is behaving correctly anyway. A technique for doing this is called jailing.

7.17. Research on Security

Computer security is a very hot topic, with a great deal of research taking place One important topic is trusted computing, especially platforms for it (Erickson, 2003; Garfinkel et al., 2003; Reid and Caelli, 2005; and Thibadeau, 2006) and public policy issues associated with it (Anderson, 2003). Information flow models and implementation is an ongoing research topic (Castro et al., 2006; Efstathopoulos et al., 2005; Hicks et al., 2007; and Zeldovich et al., 2006)

User authentication (including biometrics) is still quite important (BhargavSpantzel et al, 2006; Bergadano et al., 2002; Pusara and Bradley, 2004; Sasse, 2007; and Yoon et al., 2004).

Given all the problems with malware these days, there is a lot of research on buffer overflows and other exploits and how to deal with them (Hackett et al., 2006; Jones, 2007; Kuperman et al., 2005; Le and Soffa, 2007; and Prasad and Chiueh, 2003). Malware in all its forms is widely studied, including Trojan horses (Agrawal et al., 2007; Franz, 2007; and Moffie et al., 2006), Viruses (Bruschi et al., 2007; Cheng et al, 2007; and Rieback et al, 2006), worms (Abdelhafez et al., 2007; Jiang and Xu, 2006; Kienzle and Elder, 2003; and Tang and Chen, 2007), spy ware (Egele et al, 2007; Felten and Halderman, 2006; and Wu et al, 2006), and rootkits (Kruegel et al, 2004; Levine et al, 2006; Quynh and Takefuji, 2007; and Wang and Dasgupta, 2007). Since viruses, spyware, and rootkits all try to hide, there has been work on stealth technology and how they can be detected anyway (Carpenter et al, 2007; Garfinkei et al, 2007; and Lyda and Hamrock, 2007).

Steganography itself has also been examined (Harmsen and Pearlman, 2005; and Kratzer et al, 2006). Needless to say, there has been much work on defending systems against malware. Some of it focusing on antivirus software (Henchiri and Japkowicz, 2006; Sanok, 2005; Stiegler et al, 2006; and Uluski et al, 2005). Intrusion detection systems are an especially hot topic, with work going on about both real-time and historical intrusions (King and Chen, 2005; 2006; Saidi, 2007; Wang et al, 2006b; and Wheeler and Fulp, 2007). Honeypots are naturally an important aspect of IDSes and get quite a bit of attention themselves (Anagnostakis et al, 2005; Asrigo et al, 2006; Portokalidis et al, 2006)

7.18. Summary

Security, must consider both the computer system and the environment-people, buildings, businesses, valuable objects, and threats-within which the system is used. The data stored in the computer system must be protected from unauthorized access, malicious destruction or alteration, and accidental introduction of inconsistency. It is easier to protect against accidental loss of data consistency than to protect against malicious access to the data. Absolute protection of the information stored in a computer system from malicious abuse is not possible; but the cost to the perpetrator can be made sufficiently high to deter most, if not all, attempts to access that information without proper authority. Several types of attacks can be launched against programs and against individual computers or the masses. Stack- and buffer-overflow techniques allow successful attackers to change their level of system access. Viruses and worms are self-perpetuating, sometimes infecting thousands of computers. Denial-of-service attacks prevent legitimate use of target systems. Encryption limits the domain of receivers of data, while authentication limits the domain of senders. Encryption is used to provide confidentiality of data being stored or transferred. Symmetric encryption requires a shared key, while asymmetric encryption provides a public key and a private key. Authentication, when combined with hashing, can prove that data have not been changed. User authentication methods are used to identify legitimate users of a system. In addition to standard user-name and password protection, several authentication methods are used. One-time passwords, for example, change from session to session to avoid replay attacks. Two-factor authentication requires two forms of authentication, such as a hardware calculator with activation PIN. Multi-factor authentication uses three or more forms. These methods greatly decrease the chance of authentication forgery. Methods of preventing or detecting security incidents include intrusion detection systems, antivirus software, auditing and logging of system events, monitoring of system software changes, system-call monitoring, and firewalls.

www.ingramcontent.com/pod-product-compliance
Lightning Source LLC
Chambersburg PA
CBHW071955150726
47999CB00001B/446